The Project Manager's Communication Toolkit

The Project Manager's Communication Toolkit

Shankar Jha

CRC Press
Taylor & Francis Group
Boca Raton London New York

CRC Press is an imprint of the
Taylor & Francis Group, an **informa** business
AN AUERBACH BOOK

CRC Press
Taylor & Francis Group
6000 Broken Sound Parkway NW, Suite 300
Boca Raton, FL 33487-2742

First issued in paperback 2019

© 2010 by Taylor & Francis Group, LLC
CRC Press is an imprint of Taylor & Francis Group, an Informa business

No claim to original U.S. Government works

ISBN-13: 978-1-4398-0995-2 (hbk)
ISBN-13: 978-0-367-38432-6 (pbk)

Library of Congress Cataloging-in-Publication Data

Jha, Shankar.
  The project manager's communication toolkit / author, Shankar Jha.
    p. cm.
  "A CRC title."
  Includes index.
  ISBN 978-1-4398-0995-2 (hardcover : alk. paper)
  1. Project management. 2. Communication in management. I. Title.

T56.8.J45 2010
658.4′04--dc22

2009044678

Visit the Taylor & Francis Web site at
http://www.taylorandfrancis.com

and the CRC Press Web site at
http://www.crcpress.com

Contents

Foreword ix

Acknowledgments xi

Introduction... xiii

About the Author xvii

1   Communication: Challenges and Opportunities for Project Managers.1
Communication Concepts...2
    Types of Project Communications 3

2   Text-Based Plans, Reports, Messages, and Presentations.................11
Project Charter 12
Statement of Work..15
Project Initiation Document 17
Project Kickoff Meeting Agenda 19
Project Management Plan..21
Scope Management Plan...24
Schedule Management Plan..26
Cost Management Plan 30
Human Resource (HR) Management Plan 34
Communication Management Plan...35
Change Management Plan...38
Defect Management Plan 39
Quality Management Plan...43
Risk Management Plan... 46
    Strategies for Risk Response Planning 48
        Strategy for Threat...48
        Strategy for Opportunity..49
        Strategy for Threats and Opportunities 50
    Supporting Project Management Plans 50
        Procurement Management Plan..50
        Configuration Management (CM) Plan 52

Knowledge Management (KM) Plan 55
Transition Plan 57
Environmental Management Plan (EMP) 59
Change Request Document 60
Project Status Report 62
Milestone Report 65
Meeting Agenda and Meeting Minutes Document 66
Project Closure Report..72
Lessons Learned Document...74
Email Etiquette..76
Microsoft® PowerPoint® 82

3   Charts, Graphs, and Diagrams..85
Gantt Chart...86
Flowchart...91
S Curve..93
Column Chart..95
Resource Histogram 96
Run Chart 98
Pareto Chart 100
Cause-and-Effect Diagram 102
Pie Chart 103
Control Chart...105
How to Interpret Out-of-Control Indicators..........................108
Organization Chart 110
Work Breakdown Structure (WBS) 111
Decision Tree Diagram..113
Additional Project Schedule Reporting Tools..................................117

4   Tables and Matrices...119
Responsibility Assignment Matrix (RAM) 119
Role and Responsibility Matrix..122
Communication Matrix..124
Project Team Roster...124
Risk Probability–Impact Matrix 126
Risk Register..129
Requirements Traceability Matrix (RTM)...............................132
Quality Matrix 135
Issue Log...138
Project Dashboard 142
Pivot Table..144

5   Conclusion and Case Studies 157
Scenarios on the Usage of Text-Based Tools....................................159

Scenarios on the Usage of Chart-, Graph-, and Diagram-Based Tools 166
Scenarios on the Usage of Tables and Matrix-Based Tools 167
Miscellaneous Scenarios on the Usage of More than One Category of
Tools..170

Index **179**

Foreword

Communication is the root of virtually all success. Even engineers and mathematicians must find a way to translate their work into understandable communications for their work to be applied outside their own level of expertise.

The *project management* arena is no less dependent on successful and effective communications. However, these skills can sometimes be ignored or relegated to a back seat in favor of more "mechanical" emphasis on certification in the technical mechanisms of project management via the PMP (Project Management Professional) and other certifications.

Communications, however, are anything but mechanical, and some would say that experience is the only method for developing those skills because unlike many other tools in the project manager's toolkit, communications are inherently ambiguous and prone to interpretation. And it is interpretation—incorrect interpretation especially—that is the root cause of many project failures. From "That's not how I thought it would look" to "We're 90 percent complete—for the fourth week in a row," it is the use of more effective *two-way* communication that well could have avoided many disappointments and outright failures.

Fortunately for us, Shankar Jha has recognized and interestingly addressed the project management communications "problem" in simple, accessible, and implementable ways. Shankar's coverage of the subject presents methods and devices that can help both the developing project manager avoid years of trial-and-error experience, and help experienced project managers hone their skills for even higher levels of performance and success through more effective project management communications.

I hope you enjoy the book and find the content both interesting and useful.

R. Emory Heisler, PMP
Vice President, AmeriChoice Inc., a UHG company

Acknowledgments

I may have walked this journey alone, but the path was made easy by many individuals at various junctures. The end result would certainly have been different in the absence of their support, guidance, and extraordinary help.

John Wyzalek, the acquiring editor, was the first to identify the value of my work. He guided me in shaping the style, content, and boundaries of the book. His critical review of the sample manuscript and the valuable suggestions thereafter went a long way in making it the material it is now. Amy Blalock was quite helpful with the questions and clarifications related to the format of the manuscript and the details of other deliverables. She was always approachable and very quick with her responses.

I would like to thank Emory Heisler, Nancy Couture, Karen Davis, and Anang Srinivas for the time they spent reviewing the manuscript and providing valuable feedback. Karen has years of experience in managing the PMO and I learned a lot under her guidance. Many, many thanks to Karen for the tremendous encouragement she provided. Sonali Dixit provided a professional touch to many diagrams in this book, and I am grateful to her for all the artwork.

My wife, Mamta, has been a constant source of support throughout the span of this project. Apart from providing a tranquil environment, she also reviewed my proposal and made some great suggestions. I had complete liberty to focus on the project whenever I had to, and she took good care of our two children without ever complaining. She enjoys doing the thankless job relentlessly. There have been numerous friends, colleagues, co-workers, and my close ones, who, over the years have positively influenced my learning, development, and thought leadership. It is impossible to name each and every one of them, but this book is a tribute to all of them. Last but not the least, I would like to thank and acknowledge the Project Management Institute (PMI) for approval to reproduce its PMI content.

Introduction

People might wonder why most professionals fail to make good project managers even though they have years of industry experience in a management role and possess excellent general communication skills. You most likely have seen team leads and functional managers made project managers, and most of them fail miserably through no fault of their own. The answer lies in the unique nature of the demands of the project management profession, particularly project communication skill, which are very different from general communication skills. I have found my fellow project managers struggling to find the right communication tools for the right occasion; and even if they are aware of them, they are not comfortable using them effectively. For example, almost every project manager is aware of the Gantt chart, but how many of them use this tool under different circumstances to make communication better and to fetch a favorable result? Similarly, the S curve is a very powerful and useful tool for reporting but very few project managers use it. When plotted properly, it provides management with multiple pieces of critical information on project performance, such as scope, cost (or effort), and schedule, all in one graph. Although many are aware of these tools, they hesitate to use them because they have not seen live examples.

Often people get confused between *project schedule* and *project plan*, and their idea of project plan is quite vague and blurred. Does your organization have a clear-cut definition of a project charter, a statement of work, and a project management plan? If yes, how many project managers understand them and use them appropriately and effectively? Sometimes, team members expect that all the details of the project plan will be available on day one of the project. Imagine the impact of this confusion on the overall communication in the project. There is also a lot of misunderstanding with regard to scope. Scope is narrowly defined and understood among the project team and the stakeholders. The definition of scope goes beyond the description of the final product and services. Similarly, not many people have clarity about what change control is, and how and when it should be practiced. This results in loose control over the project parameters and causes a tremendous amount of conflict in the project. In general, people do not clearly understand what a risk is, and how it is different from an issue. Naturally, they are ill prepared to handle the risks and issues. Seldom do companies have strong processes, procedures, and guidelines for dealing with project risk. This has a huge impact on projects, and nobody really understands why the projects turn into red and the team continues to work in firefighting mode until the project comes to a screeching halt after months of chaos and confusion. The blame game does not stop; the heads roll but the real problem is never addressed.

As a person gains experience and climbs the ladder of corporate hierarchy, he/she learns these tricks and tools through training or by following company standards, procedures, and processes and by learning from peers and senior personnel. But often the learning process is slow and comes in a hard way. Many project managers, who spend years in the profession, struggle to find the right tools for the right occasion. Although they have all the information available to them, their reports still look shoddy and cause dissatisfaction among stakeholders for lack of better visual presentation. People work extra hard on their presentations, messages, and reports but still the outcome is not satisfactory most of the time. They fail to understand why audiences do not read their reports and messages on time; and when they are read, they are not well understood; and when responded to, they cause communication overhead for many. There are circumstances when you need to communicate a very important message to a group of selected people. This message has a lot of content and you need a prompt response from some key players. You have made a substantial effort in compiling the message. But to your dismay, very few key players reply to it on time; and for those who respond, they confuse you even more. And then, a chain of emails starts flying around, engulfing everyone in a maze of miscommunication and utter confusion. With the right communication skills, you can avoid this unnecessary noise from the first place. The project might be in a deep crisis, but there are project managers who write and present a report in such a way that it makes them and their team look diligent, smart, and hard working—not only in the eyes of their own management, but also in the eyes of customers, users, and other stakeholders. On the other hand, if a report is shoddy, then no matter how good the status of the project is on the ground level and how well the project manager has managed the project, the project manager will end up in conflicts and will earn the wrath of stakeholders.

Projects fail primarily because of communication lapses. Because project managers own the responsibility of communication management, it is critical that they truly understand the nuances of this trade. Considering the criticality of effective and efficient communication during the project and the observations mentioned above, I was prompted to write this book so that I can reach a wider audience and help them become better professionals, gain greater job satisfaction, and advance their careers. This book will help readers address the practical difficulties in their day-to-day project communication. There are books that explain what a tool is and how to create it, but this book also explains how the tool should be used in different real-life situations. Just knowing about the tool is not sufficient; one can use it only once one understands when and how the tool should be used. This book is unlike so many others that are filled with myriad theoretical concepts; readers will find this book practical, to the point, and valuable—yet short and enchanting enough to finish in a few sittings.

About the Author

Shankar Jha, PMP, has more than twelve years of managerial experience at various levels, with eight years as a project and program manager working with some large multinational companies. Over the past six years, Shankar has anchored and provided training on project management topics to a large number of project managers, team leads, resource managers, and other employees.

Shankar began his career in project management with one of the most respected Indian multinational companies; there he successfully managed process improvements, value addition initiatives, knowledge management, and quality improvement initiatives apart from managing client projects. Later he moved on to work with an American multinational where he managed projects, programs, and engagements for a Fortune 100 client.

Shankar holds an undergraduate degree (Bachelor of Technology in Mining Engineering) from a premier and nationally renowned institute (ISM, Dhanbad) in India. He continued to update his knowledge by acquiring various relevant certifications and by attending training programs in-house as well as outside. He is a member of the American Management Association, and he has been a member of the Project Management Institute and Institute of Engineers (India) in the past. Currently Shankar is working for Cognizant Technology Solutions; before this, he worked for Tata Steel (world's second most geographically diversified steel producer and one of the world's top five steel producers) and Infosys Technology Ltd.

Chapter 1

Communication: Challenges and Opportunities for Project Managers

There is an old adage: "It is not what you say, but how you say it." A fact can be communicated in several ways; however, good communication not only resolves conflicts and solves problems, but also makes an ordinary work effort look extraordinary, bringing out the best returns to the presenter. You may have heard the joke about smoking while praying.

> Two friends are walking to a religious service. The first friend wonders whether it would be all right to smoke while praying. The second friend says, "Why don't you ask the priest?"
> So the first friend goes up to the priest and asks, "Father, may I smoke while I pray?"
> The priest replies, "Oh no, my son, you should not! That is disrespect to God. That is sinful and outrageous."
> He goes back to his friend and tells him what the priest advised. His friend says, "I am not surprised. You asked the wrong question. Let me try." And so the second friend goes up to the priest and asks, "Father, may I pray while I smoke?"

To which the priest happily replies, "Absolutely, my son! Absolutely! You can always pray whenever and wherever you want to."

According to Peter Drucker, the ability to communicate well is essential for success and is perhaps the most important of all the skills an individual should possess. Tom Peter says that "Communication is everyone's panacea for everything." A high percentage of the friction, frustrations, and inefficiencies in working relationships are traceable to poor communication. There is no denying the fact that good communication is an essential skill for the success of a management professional in any business, and it is even more important in a project environment. However, communication needs are very different in a project compared to any other business environment and so, apart from the general communication tools, it also requires the familiarity and mastery of a specific set of tools suited for the specific need. Projects are becoming more and more complex because of the changing business circumstances, such as multivendor organizations, matrix organizations, multicultural workforces, offshore–onsite models, global delivery models, remote locations, etc. With growing global competition, there is more pressure on organizations to finish projects on time and within budget. This leads to higher expectations from stakeholders and therefore creates more chances of conflicts. Thus, communication challenges are growing day by day.

Projects mostly fail because of communication breakdown. Project managers play the role of communication coordinator and thus they are responsible for both the success and failure of communication inside the project. In general, project managers (PMs) spend 90 percent of their time in communication. No wonder why communication skill is the single most desirable skill of a PM. PMs can face challenges from all quarters—high expectations from senior management, unrealistic deadlines, scope creep, resource competition, unknown risks, uncertain dependencies, insufficient team skill, lack of accountability from key team members, conflicting interests among stakeholders, internal politics, and weak organizational processes and methodologies—just to name a few. Often these challenges show up in groups and can drive any normal PM crazy. But the PMs can successfully handle these situations with the help of good communication skills. Just as soldiers must possess the weapons and equipment to fight under different circumstances and must master the art and science of those weapons, so too a project manager must be aware of the right kinds of tools and techniques to fight the all-important communication battle.

Let us understand some basic concepts of communication in general and how it is defined and conceptualized specific to projects.

Communication Concepts

Communication is as old as human beings. It is perhaps older than civilization and it is older than the oldest language ever existed on earth. Communication is part and parcel of every living entity's life. We perform some kind of communication all the time, but yet communication skill is elusive to most people. Human beings invented, cultured, and nurtured so many different languages, dialects, grammars, scripts, signals, mediums, channels, tools, and technologies to make communication better, easier, simpler, and more convenient. Ironically, it has become more and more complex. In the modern world, communication, along with its numerous branches and subbranches, has become a vast area of research. With advancing technologies, changing social patterns, increasing global human interactions, and rising business competition, new aspects are constantly being added to communication. Readers must have come across terms such as "linguistic communication," "paralinguistic communication," "interpersonal communication," "anomalous communication," "psychic communication," "auditory communication, verbal communication, nonverbal communication, written communication," "mass communication," "telecommunication," etc. The list goes on and on—it is mind boggling.

Over time, many scholars, scientists, social scientists, and psychologists have attempted to define communication from different angles and different perspectives. But in its simplest form it can be defined through a sender–receiver model (see Figure 1.1). In this model, a sender transfers a message containing information to a receiver. This is the activity of conveying information. More elaborately, it can be defined as the exchange of thoughts, messages, or information, as by speech, signal, writing, or behavior.

Types of Project Communications

1. *Interpersonal communication:* This is a very important and necessary skill for the project manager and includes listening, self-presentation, problem solving, decision making, negotiating, and conflict management. The goals of interpersonal communications include:
   - Understanding the exact meaning and intent of others
   - Being understood by others

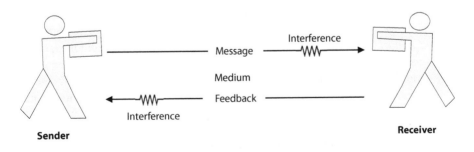

Figure 1.1 Sender–receiver model.

  – Gaining acceptance for yourself and your ideas
  – Producing action and change
2. *Communication with public and community:* Includes all public relationship efforts necessary to encourage community involvement, enhance public understanding of the project, break down resistance, gain acceptance, and perform the role of the spokesperson for the project.
3. *Formal communication:* This is mostly done through written communication and includes plans, reports, memos, letters, forms, guidelines, etc.
4. *Informal communication:* This kind of communication is generally done through face-to-face or other verbal channels and is dependent on common interests, hobbies, kinship, social status, social background, etc.

One should not confuse communication skills with project management communications. Communication skill and the art of communication are broader in scope than project management communications. The art of communications includes the following:

■ Sender–receiver model.
■ Choice of media: When to communicate in writing versus orally, when to write an informal memo versus a formal report, when to communicate face to face versus email. The media chosen for communication activities will depend on the situation.
■ Writing style: Active versus passive voice, sentence structure, and word choice.
■ Presentation techniques: Body language and design of visual aids.
■ Meeting management techniques: Preparing an agenda and dealing with conflict.

Following are some key terms involved in the sender–receiver model, and their definition. This will help readers understand the communication model better.

■ *Sender:* The originator of the message; the source of communication, also known as communicator.
■ *Receiver:* The person for whom the message is intended.
■ *Message:* Data that is encoded by the sender and decoded by the receiver.
■ *Channel:* The medium by which the information is transmitted; for example, paper or electronic communication. There is a very nice quotation on communication medium by Simone Weil that sums up the important role of medium in any communication. (http://www.saidwhat.co.uk/topicquote/communication [July 10, 2008]).

"Two prisoners whose cells adjoin communicate with each other by knocking on the wall. The wall is the thing which separates them but is also their means of communication. Every separation is a link."

- *Encode:* To translate thoughts and ideas into a language that is understood by others.
- *Decode:* To translate message back into the meaningful thoughts.
- *Noise:* Any interference or disturbance that confuses the message (e.g., distance).
- *Communication barrier:* Obstacles that impede communications (e.g., limited communication channels, distance, noise, cultural differences, organizational climate, perceptions, limited information, withholding of information, terminology, hidden agenda, etc.).
- *Filtering:* Occurs when a large portion of the message is lost between the sender and the receiver. It is generally caused by language problems, cultural differences, semantics, lack of knowledge base, etc.

The components of the sender–receiver model (Figure 1.1) must be taken into account when dealing with interpersonal communications during project communications. There are many challenges in using these components to effectively communicate with project stakeholders. To ensure that messages are received and understood, two-way communication is necessary. The sender determines what information to share and with whom to share it. Next, the sender encodes the message before transmitting through the medium to the receiver as a signal. The receiver receives the message, decodes to understand its meaning, and then responds accordingly. Communication is successful if the decoded message is the same as the sender intended it. Using experience, the sender anticipates how the message will be decoded and encodes the message accordingly. Both the sender and receiver have a duty to understand and to be understood. This is accomplished through feedback and acknowledgment.

The PM should have an understanding of the barriers to successful communication. Examples of some common communication barriers include information overload, lack of subject knowledge, cultural differences, organizational environment, preoccupied notion, and large number of communication links. It is very important to understand the effect of the number of links in any communication. The following formula is widely used to calculate the number of links in the communication:

$$\text{Number of links} = n(n - 1)/2$$

where n is the number of people involved in communication.

For example, if you are communicating with just one person, then the number of people involved is two. Using the above formula, the number of links in this case will be one only. If you are communicating with two other people, then the number of links will be three. If you have a total of five people involved, then the number of links becomes ten. Similarly, if you have ten people in the loop, then the number of links suddenly rises to forty-five. Therefore, if you plan to send a communication to ten people, then expect the message to be repeated at least forty-five times. The communication link grows in a nonlinear fashion as you add more participants. The repetition of the communication has a huge negative impact on the project, especially if the original message was not clear and to the point. Imagine the impact of any mistake in communication where many people are involved. So, plan all the messages properly in terms of their recipients and always think twice before adding extra participants to any communication.

There are three forms of communication: verbal, nonverbal, and written. Nonverbal communication includes gestures, vocal tones, facial expression, environmental settings, manner of dress, and body language. In general, nonverbal factors have more influence on the total impact of the message than do verbal factors. According to Albert Meharabian, words account for only 7 percent, whereas vocal tone contributes 38 percent and facial expression contributes 55 percent in a face-to-face communication (http://en.wikipedia.org/wiki/Albert_Mehrabian [June 30, 2008]). The PM is the leader of the project, so he/she must be very careful with the nonverbal form of the communication so that he/she sends out clear and unambiguous messages. To be effective, mean what you say and say what you mean. This is called *walking the talk*. In the context of a project, written communication includes plans, reports, guidelines, procedures, messages, presentations, and other forms of information distribution to the stakeholders. The corresponding tools form the basis of the PM's communication. This book focuses on the PM's needs of written communication and provides practical tips about various common or uncommon tools. On the one hand this book serves as an eye-opener to some useful project communication management tools, and on the other hand it also provides tips through real-life examples and easy-to-understand language to make the reading easier and understanding better. Tools in this book are categorized into three basic types: (1) text-based plans, reports, messages, and presentations (see Chapter 2); (2) charts, graphs, and diagrams (see Chapter 3); and (3) tables and matrices (see Chapter 4).

Communication planning and execution can be difficult, especially if you are new to the organization and you do not know the stakeholders and their expectations well. Initial days are very critical in building relationships and rapport with different customers and the clients. If the expectations are not understood and the communication is not planned properly, then the project managers often struggle to communicate the project information effectively. They either send too many reports or produce status reports that make little sense to most of the stakeholders. They generate too few reports and do not provide a complete and satisfactory picture of the project. However, they can get better over time if they seriously observe the pattern, feedback, and comments from the key stakeholders. Understand the risk tolerance level of the key stakeholders and the customers. Customers with a high risk tolerance level are easy to deal with, and they require less reports and updates compared to those who have medium and low levels of risk tolerance. People with high risk tolerance levels are more positive and are usually more optimistic. Stakeholders with a low risk tolerance level will try to avert any risk, will ask too many questions, will indulge in micromanagement, and then you will be required to have more and frequent communication with such customers. Communication problems occur throughout the life of the project; planning makes life easy. These problems have a huge impact on the project. It is essential to plan for the communication so that communication-related problems can be approached proactively and the project manager is prepared for any situation. Most project managers either knowingly ignore or struggle in this discipline. Sometimes they are oblivious to this important aspect of project management. There can be many reasons for this, including:

1. Weak organizational process often leads to this problem. People generally tend to follow the processes of the organization and they ignore anything that they are not formally required to do. So, if formal communication planning is not part of the organizational process, then project managers overlook this important aspect of their job.
2. Project managers take this task for granted and do not allocate enough time for the task. They consider other planning tasks as more important and get busy with them, and later they never find time to return to this important task. Sometimes they ignore planning for this task due to overconfidence. They think that they have been dealing with most of the people and stakeholders from the past assignments and thus they do not require mapping out a formal plan. But that is foolhardy and frequently leads to failure.
3. Lack of training and knowledge to carry out this task properly. They lack the skill and experience to initiate and carry out this task. Most project managers do not understand how to proceed with communication planning and so they hesitate doing so.

Details of the project communication tools are provided in the following chapters. Some common best practices are listed below; in general they should be performed by the project managers to prevent most communication problems.

1. Solicit inputs, prepare the project status report, and distribute it on a scheduled day and time. In general, the status report is distributed on either Friday or Monday. This establishes a rhythm and creates confidence among the stakeholders.
2. Hold weekly meeting with the key stakeholders of the project. This is very important because many times you will observe that your effort of producing the status report goes to waste because people are not reading the report. You may end up sending the same information multiple times to different people. This situation can be avoided if everybody goes through the report at once and asks all the questions for you to answer once. The process will ensure that everyone is on the same page and you can save valuable time for yourself. Sometimes, an important point can go unnoticed unless you discuss it directly with the stakeholders.

3. Hold a weekly project status meeting with all project team members. Also invite the functional managers. This is a very important tool for project communication. Some team members may argue that they only speak for two minutes but they have to spend an entire hour in the meeting, so it is a waste of their time. But one should realize that the project is a coordinated effort and everyone should be aware of the "big picture" and what is going on in the project. Others' work or a decision about others' work may have an impact on that particular team member's work; and if the status and issues are discussed separately, then synergy cannot be achieved. Apart from this, there can be so many generic communications and other project agendas to be discussed as a group. Team meetings enhance the sense of belonging and strengthen teamwork.

4. Send out the meeting agenda at least a couple of hours before the meeting. At the same time, the gap between the agenda distribution and the meeting should not be more than a day.

5. Send minutes of the meeting preferably the same day; if not possible, then the following day. A delay in sending minutes might cause a delay in the intensity and in the activities related to action items.

6. Hold a daily checkpoint meeting when the project is in the Quality Testing phase. This is the point when the project is close to implementation. It is very important to keep track of all the defects and issues, and then follow up every day so that defect-fix turnaround can be quicker and the intensity can be maintained.

7. Hold meetings twice a week with subject matter experts and team leads when the project is in the Analysis phase.

8. Communicate project schedule to the entire team on a regular basis and keep reminding them of the upcoming milestones. The schedule should be updated at least on a weekly basis, indicating percent completion, changes in any dates, addition or removal of tasks, etc.

9. In most cases, you may not own the project human resources. In matrix organizations, the human resources report to their functional managers and so you may not have any direct reports. When a resource issue arises, try to work with the respective functional manager and always keep the manager in the loop for major decisions impacting their resources. If the deliverables are not completed on time or if you have behavioral issues with any resource or any other resource conflict, resolve these issues with the help of the resource manager. It is your duty to raise the issue in a timely manner so that the resource manager can take corrective action.

Before understanding the project communication tools, let us understand a couple of basic project management terms that are used quite often in this book. There are five project management process groups and nine project management knowledge areas. These process groups are initiating, planning, executing, monitoring and control, and closing. Process groups are different from process phases, so one should not consider them the same. The number of phases depends on the organization's project management process, which can vary. However, there are always five process groups, which occur multiple times in a project. All five process groups take place at least once in every phase of the project. The nine knowledge areas include:

1. Project integration management
2. Project scope management
3. Project time management
4. Project cost management
5. Project quality management
6. Project human resource management
7. Project communications management
8. Project risk management
9. Project procurement management

Knowledge areas are nothing but specialized disciplines within the project management domain. Every knowledge area has separate processes, inputs, tools and techniques, and outputs. All five project management processes are performed within every knowledge area.

Chapter 2

Text-Based Plans, Reports, Messages, and Presentations

Project managers use text-based communication tools most of the time. Text is best suited for providing background information, narrating stories, explaining processes, providing step-by-step procedures for tasks, writing memos, and compiling reports. Tables, graphs, and/or diagrams are often included as a supplement or attachment to reports, plans, memos, and presentations. This chapter lists and explains a variety of tools owned by project managers. They are discussed from the point of view of their contents, their relationship with each other, and the purpose they serve for the project. Sometimes people cannot distinguish or differentiate among the various tools and they often become confused about the document/tool by looking at the contents of these documents, such as the project management plan, project charter, Statement of Work (SOW), and project initiation document, and they assume that these documents are one and the same. However, there are big differences among these tools. This chapter explains those differences and also gives an idea about the timing when they are prepared and updated within a project life cycle. Most organizations have templates for these plans, reports, and other types of documents. Project managers need to use those templates and, if required, can make suitable modifications to meet the needs and expectations of the project and the stakeholders. Some tools provide an opportunity for a freestyle writing. Emails and presentations, most often, do not have any templates, so project managers are free to format them the way they want. Emails are the lifeline of business communication these days, so one must be aware of email etiquette and practice it appropriately to become a more effective communicator and a better professional.

Project Charter

The Project Management Institute (PMI) defines a project charter as a document that formally authorizes a project. It is also referred to as the *project definition report, project definition document,* and *terms of reference.* The charter authorizes the project manager to apply organizational resources to project activities. A project initiator, sponsor, or business owner, external to the project organization, generally issues the project charter. The sponsor or owner is usually part of the senior management. The intent of a project charter is to give notice of the new project and new project manager, and to demonstrate upper management support for the project and the project manager. The project charter primarily documents the business needs, project justification, customer requirements, and new products and services that are intended to satisfy customer requirements. Many organizations—and sometimes small projects—do not have a formal charter document. The scope statement often satisfies the need for a charter with emails/memos declaring approval and PM authority. A project scope document, if one exists, is usually attached to the project charter. The project charter, either directly or by reference to other documents (such as RFP, SOW, contract document), should address the following information:

1. Project name and project number.
2. Name of the project sponsor, who prepared the charter, and the date when it was last updated.
3. Name of the project manager, responsibilities and authority: Depending on the structure of the organization, the responsibility and authority of the project manager may vary.
4. Business needs, high-level project description, or product requirements that the project is being undertaken to address.
5. Project purpose. This section answers the question: Why does the project exist? The organization's business need can be based on market demand, technological advance, customer request, legal requirement, and/or a social need. Define the objectives of the project as they relate to the goals and objectives of the organization. Identify the organization's strategic goals that this project will support; and for each goal, identify the project objectives. Figure 2.1 shows this mapping. The project plan to be developed later will have a project performance measurement plan to measure the performance against each of these goals and objectives.
6. Customer requirements: These are the requirements that satisfy customer, sponsor, and other stakeholder needs, wants, and expectations. This section should clearly state, on a high level, what is inside and what is outside the

Organizations Strategic Goals	Project Objectives

Figure 2.1   Strategic goals and project objectives.

scope of the project. It sets the limits or boundaries of the project. A good scope definition avoids scope creep in the later stages. It is also important to establish the difference between the necessary components and deliverables and those that are desirable but not absolutely necessary. Defining needs and wants is an excellent way to define the scope of a project and to set the parameters for project planning. It can be a catalyst for discussion about what is really needed from the project, and it can force realistic decisions about what can and cannot be done.

7. Milestone schedule: At this point, only the major milestones are available; the project team should elaborate the detail. Sometimes, the project charter may just have start and end dates.

8. Budget summary: At this point, you will only have the overall budget for the project. Later on, during the project planning phase, you can elaborate the budget for every phase and also at the task level.

9. Stakeholders information: Record all stakeholders, and their organization, involved in the project and impacted by the project. Identify the roles of these organizations and stakeholders and in what capacity they will participate in the project. The project charter should identify the organization of the project steering committee, the change control board, etc.

10. Functional organizations involved: This gives the project manager and other stakeholders the idea of the functional units responsible for carrying out the project work. Some organizations may not perform the work directly but may participate in the project for some other function, such as product testing, verification, helping with logistical support, etc.

11. Assumptions: The charter documents the assumptions related to the organizational and external environments. Validate these assumptions as the project progresses, because these assumptions are potential risks to the project. Scope, quality, schedule, budget, and sometimes the viability of the project depend on the assumptions. The project may be impacted if any assumption goes wrong. This may necessitate a change request in case the scope, cost, and/or schedule is impacted directly or indirectly by the failure of one or more assumptions.

12. Constraints: Provide the basic outline of known time, cost, scope, quality, security, safety, and other constraints. Also document how flexible the scope, schedule, cost, security, and quality are.

As is evident, this document is created before the project begins but is not a static document, although it may appear as such. In a multiphase project, the outcome of a phase gets validated against the decisions made in the original charter, and the next phase of the project gets authorized and the charter is updated, if required. The PM can actively participate in the preparation of the charter or provide support and information to the sponsor or owner who prepared the document.

The project charter is the first official document of the project because it authorizes the project and sets the project in motion. This is neither a scope document nor a project management plan. The charter provides a definition of almost all aspects of the project on a very high level. It is kind of a project summary, which is ideal for presentation to upper management, customers, and other stakeholders. The document describes what is to be done, not how it is to be done. The entire contents are at the summary level. Project managers take this information, further elaborate some information themselves, and obtain further elaboration from the project team members. For example, the PM is responsible for taking the charter as input and preparing the detailed project plan, project schedule, project budget details, project organization chart, etc. At the same time, other functional leads will be responsible for detailing the scope, architecture, design solutions, test plan, etc. Based on input from the charter, the PM understands the functional organizations involved in the project, interacts with the leads of these organizations, and understands who will represent these organizations on the project. It is advisable to set up meetings with the project sponsor and the business owner, and invite the leads to understand the project. This can be done through multiple sessions based on the complexity and size of the project and also on the familiarity of the PM and the team leads with the business function. Scope, assumptions, constraints, and other information are understood and validated in these meetings. If needed, the project charter can be revised and updated following these transition and review sessions. During the initial days, the PM and team members refer to the project charter as the main guiding document. The project team should first concentrate on understanding the project by going through the project charter and reviewing it critically. Sometimes people may get so enthusiastic that they jump in to discuss the solution. This should be avoided. At this time, project team members should focus on understanding the project and its different aspects to figure out what the needs, wants, and expectations of the customer and the sponsor are. The PM is responsible for keeping the team focused on the job. So, this is a very important document for the project team in the beginning. If the customer or the sponsor has not put enough time and effort into documenting the project charter, then the project team may have to spend a significant amount of time figuring out the details. This might pose a risk to the project; so be cognizant of this risk and discuss it with the sponsor in an effort to detail the information appropriately to facilitate an easy and correct understanding of the project.

Statement of Work

The PMI defines a Statement of Work (SOW) as a narrative description of products or services to be supplied by the project. For internal projects, the project initiator or sponsor provides the SOW based on business needs, product, or service requirements. For external projects, the SOW can be received from the customer as part of a bid document—for example, RFQ (Request for Quotation), RFP (Request for Proposal), Request for Information—or as part of a contract. An organization desiring to have the work done (i.e., the prospective customer) produces an SOW as part of an RFP. Vendors or services companies (prospective contractors) respond with Proposals. The SOW specifies requirements at a very high level. Detailed requirements and pricing are usually specified at a later stage.

Contents that are typically addressed by an SOW are as follows:

1. *Purpose Statement:* This section answers the question of why the project is being done. It also relates the organization's business need that prompted the initiation of the project. The organization's business need can be based on needed training, market demand, technological advance, legal requirement, or governmental standard.
2. *Scope of Work:* This section describes the work to be done, specifies the hardware and software involved, as well as the exact nature of the work to be done.
3. *Location of Work:* This section documents where the work will be performed. It also specifies the location of hardware and software and where people will meet to perform the work.
4. *Timelines:* This section specifies the allowable time for projects, such as start and finish times, number of hours that can be billed per week or month, where work is to be performed, and anything else that relates to scheduling.
5. *Deliverables Schedule:* This section lists the specific deliverables, describing what is due and when it is due.
6. *Applicable Standards:* This section describes any industry-specific standards that must be adhered to in fulfilling the contract.
7. *Acceptance Criteria:* This section specifies how the buyer or receiver of goods and services will determine if the product or service is acceptable, and what criteria will be used to state that the work is acceptable. These provide input into the critical success factors for the project and help in setting up quality goals. Project scheduling details and costing details will take input from this information.

8. *Assumptions and Risks:* This section details all the assumptions that the organization is making for different components of the project. Information on known risk should also be documented in the SOW.
9. *Constraints:* This section documents all the constraints related to schedule, cost, scope, quality, security, etc. It should also document how the deviation should be handled. This may be related to the acceptance criteria.
10. *Special Requirements:* This section specifies any special hardware or software, specialized workforce requirements, such as degrees or certifications for personnel, travel requirements, and anything else not covered in the contract specifics.

The SOW can be very lengthy and may include other information such as contract terms and conditions, pricing details, warranty coverage, technical requirements, list of deliverables, milestones, change control processes, etc. The above description of the SOW may give an impression that it is not prepared by the PM. This is partially true; in many cases, the PM will end up creating the SOW or assisting in developing this document, particularly if the project requires services from a vendor or contractor. The SOW is sometimes also called the *project proposal document.* When project proposals are required, it is often the business group that owns the project and creates the proposal document. Sometimes the PM is not assigned to the project because this document may be required too early in the life of the project. Often, the proposal may not even materialize in a project, so it would be premature to assign a PM. Typically, it also depends on the process of the organization. Depending on the company and the legal complications of the proposal, a legal team and upper management take part in the documentation of the SOW. The procurement department or the vendor management department may actively participate in the SOW preparation process. Note that the SOW is a one-time document and once signed off, it should not be changed.

Sufficient planning and effort should go into the preparation of the SOW document because it is a tool for communication with the outside organization and usually becomes part of the contract. If the information is not complete and clear, then it can become a major source of conflict and friction, perhaps leading to legal ramifications. Ensure that all the parties understand the SOW word for word and, if needed, perform multiple rounds of revisions before locking in the document for the project proposal to be signed and the work to commence. Upper management, project sponsor, project manager, team members, contractors, and subcontractors should critically review and re-review the document. It is crucial to add all known issues in the document to ensure that the bidding companies do not miss anything while responding to the proposal. It would be unfair to any bidding company to leave out known issues and concerns that might affect their delivery of work. One should understand that the failure of the vendor is the failure of the project that ultimately affects the organization that wants the work to get done. Missing information is fuel for friction and conflicts if not handled properly. This may lead to multiple and costly change requests.

The SOW is used to communicate the work of the project to an outside organization for bidding purposes; it is rarely used for internal projects. The SOW is used as a guide throughout the life cycle of the project to facilitate further planning, execution, monitoring, and control, including the management of the contract. The PM of the performing organization prepares the project management plan based on this document. Because the SOW provides information on the scope of the project, it is therefore used to allow companies to bid on work, assist in the documentation of the terms and conditions of the contract, and help in responding to bidding questions. Almost all project decisions, including those related to scope, cost, schedule, quality, security, resource, safety, environment, etc., can be taken based on this document.

Project Initiation Document

"A good start is half the job done." The way a project starts sets the tone for the rest of the life of the project. So it is imperative to start the project the right way so that it creates good momentum that continues throughout the duration of the project. The project initiation document (PID) helps in achieving this goal. The PM assigned in the beginning of the project should assume the responsibility for creating a detailed PID. The business owner should ensure that this is done properly and on time, and should also review and approve the document. This document should be signed off by the project governance board before the project actually starts. The PID should be distributed to the core project team (remember that the project will have only the core team in the beginning) and other stakeholders. The precise composition of the PID will be influenced by such considerations as management attitudes and the perceived complexity of the project. A PID usually contains the following:

1. *Business case:* Details the justification for undertaking and for continuing the project. This includes the financial and other benefits that the project is expected to deliver. This can be copied directly from the project charter.
2. *Scope of the project:* This is mentioned at a high level because the detail scope is not yet available. The project team needs to elaborate the detailed scope. Again, this can be copied from the project charter.
3. *Project organization:* Once the PM is assigned, it is his/her job to meet with the functional heads, and present them with the human resource requirements at different stages of the project. Resource names for the entire team may not be available in the beginning, but the names of leads should be available. The PM should prepare the organization chart based on these details. Team leads get to know whom they are working with and then it sets the ball rolling from there.

4. *Customer and vendor organization:* It is important for the project team to understand what the organization structures of the customer and the vendor are. This will help in setting up communication channels.
5. *Cost, schedule, and other constraints:* The cost, schedule, and constraints within which the project is required to operate and against which its performance will be evaluated. It is very important that the project team leads and functional managers understand these constraints so they work accordingly. At the same time, the PM can obtain invaluable suggestions from the team to work through the obstacles and constraints.
6. *Boundary of the project:* The boundary of the project makes it clear how related projects interact, and where the output from one project forms the input to another project, or related area of work. It is very important to understand project boundaries in the beginning.
7. *High-level project plan:* Consists of Configuration Management Plan, Resource Plan, Quality Plan, Technical Plan, Communication Plan, etc. The PM may still be working on the project management plan and its various components, but he/she can come up with at least some high-level plan for the team to understand how they need to work in the project. The PM may get a lot of assistance from the PMO support staff for coming up with these documents.
8. *A framework of process to manage and control the project:* Information from historical projects provides a lot of input for this part. The deed for special processes can be mentioned here and can be discussed in initial team meetings.

The PM should exhibit a lot of confidence and enthusiasm in understanding the project, setting up processes, and facilitating meetings with outside organizations for the team members. The core team should initially meet at least two times a week, and discuss various aspects of the project, requirement understandings, architecture, testing strategies, lessons learned from similar past projects, assumptions, constraints, risks and issues, etc. Prepare a task list, also called an action item list, for the initial few weeks of the project. Action items from previous meetings can be discussed first and a new set of action items can be created and assigned to their rightful owners.

One might become confused with regard to a project charter, SOW, project proposal, contract, project plan, and PID documents because their contents are similar in many ways. However, they serve different purposes inside the project and thus should not be considered one and the same. A close look at the discussion of these documents reveals this fact. The project charter and SOW (in most cases) may not be owned by a PM in the beginning. The PM updates the project charter later as and when required. Similarly, later he might update the original SOW in case that is required. Sometimes a PM may create contract SOW if a vendor is engaged to finish some tasks or a subproject. Every organization will not have all of these documents as part of their process. Some organizations may just create an SOW and project charter; some just create a charter. The SOW and project proposal are the same. The project charter and SOW describe what the work is; the project management plan describes how the work will be done; and the project initiation document is meant only for the project team members and the project performing organization and tells them *what the work entails* and briefly describes *how the work is intended to get done.*

Project Kickoff Meeting Agenda

The SOW, the project charter, the PID; what's next? The core team is assigned and some or all of the core team members, including the PM, have already started working on the project, but the opening bell has not yet rung. A kickoff meeting is akin to formally announcing to the project team members and key stakeholders that the project is starting. This does not happen on the first day or during the first hour of the start of the project. In fact, the PM needs to do a lot of preparation before conducting this meeting. This is because of the criticality and importance of this meeting. So much has been mentioned about the importance of a good start. It is applicable everywhere, in every campaign, and in every project. A good start to anything serves as a morale booster. It is probably the first time the project team comes together, so the PM should take this as an opportunity to energize the group to achieve the common goal. This meeting creates an atmosphere of togetherness and cohesiveness, and establishes a bond. For any meeting to be successful, it needs a clear-cut direction; a good agenda helps achieve that. One can include the following in the agenda for this meeting:

1. Project number/name.
2. Project manager: In case of more than one project manager, list all the names and indicate who the lead is. If the area of responsibility is decided, then also list that.
3. Meeting date/time.
4. Meeting location/conference details: It is a good idea to have Web conferencing because participants may be located remotely or may attend from their office.
5. Participants: Include project core team, steering committee members, customers, vendors, and members of other impacted organizations. This is the first opportunity for the project team to meet with all key stakeholders in one meeting. Some team members may not have the opportunity to meet with the senior executives during the course of the project.
6. Project organization, customer organization, project governance structure and introduction of participants describing their roles and location. All team members may not be located in one place.

7. Project description: Try to draw a simple, high-level picture of what the project is going to achieve. This picture should have input, what the project is doing, and output. Draw "before" and "after" pictures to show how the end state will be once the project achieves its objective. This exercise will bring everyone to the same page and often people ask wonderful questions that help in planning, preparing risk register, etc.

8. In-scope and out-of-scope items.

9. Assumptions and constraints: By now the assumptions and constraints may have more details compared to the original project charter. Mention project budget. Apart from these, also list all the known risks and corresponding action plans.

10. Deliverables: Mention the major deliverables with which the customers are concerned. Mention and discuss the names of the owner, reviewer, and approver for each of the deliverables. Most of the deliverables will be owned by the project team or the project organization but the customer may also own a few important deliverables, such as detailed acceptance criteria document, test data, specimen against which the product will be tested, etc.

11. Milestones: Provide a tentative timeline for major milestones and deliverables. It is important to stress that timelines are tentative and based on an order-of-magnitude (OOM) estimate; also mention at what stage the timelines will be finalized. This expectation setting goes a long way toward avoiding cost- and timeline-related conflicts at a later stage.

12. Key success factors: Mention all the key success factors as listed in the project charter and the SOW. Key success factors are related to the acceptance criteria.

13. Information about project website or project library: Everyone should be aware of the place where final and interim project deliverables are stored and archived. Some people may need to request access to the project library.

14. Introduction to project management plan: Discuss the project management plan at a high level and ask the participants to go through the details and return with questions. This needs to be formally signed off. In case the project plan is not ready, this serves as a "heads-up."

15. Communication plan: It is very important to discuss this separately even though it is part of the project plan. Primarily, discuss the types of meetings to be held and the types of reports to be generated and their frequency. Stakeholders can suggest if they would like to change anything with regard to their communication needs.

16. Questions and answers: As a good practice, allow questions as you go through the topics on the agenda, but allot some time at the end of the meeting to cover most of the questions. This meeting provides an opportunity for the team members to hear directly from the customer, and vice versa. In general, the kickoff meeting should be kept to a minimum of one hour; but based on the scale and complexity of the project, it can be scheduled for an hour and a half or two hours.

Try to keep this meeting as light as possible. The project kickoff meeting generates a great deal of positive energy for the team members and the customers attending the meeting. As discussed earlier, for some team members, it may be the only opportunity to meet and hear upper management, customers, and/or the members of other organizations. So, the meeting has a lasting impact on the team members. This is the time for you to make an impression on the team members and the customers. So prepare and handle the meeting well to give a kick-start to your project. The team members should get a feeling that they have come together to work for a common and valuable cause. Make sure that all key participants from all the organizations participate in the meeting; otherwise, the purpose of the meeting is defeated. Reach out to people offline for gathering information in order to prepare for the meeting. Talk to individuals days before the meeting and if someone does not feel the meeting is necessary, then convince the person to attend. Understand the expectations of upper management and the customers well in advance; this will help in documenting and preparing for this meeting. Similarly, talk to the team members well in advance and make them understand the purpose of this meeting. Ask their expectations and if they hesitate to ask some question, then you can document the specifics and ask for them in the meeting. At the same time, some disgruntled employee may take out his/her frustrations in the meeting, so make sure you talk to that employee beforehand and explain to the purpose of the meeting. However, if such a thing happens, you can handle the situation by stopping the person politely and offering to take the matter offline.

Project Management Plan

The project management plan, sometimes simply called a *project plan,* is the most important document a project manager owns. The PMI defines project plan as a formal, *approved* document that defines how the project is executed, monitored, and controlled. The primary use of the project plan is to document planning assumptions and decisions, facilitate communication among stakeholders, and document approved scope, cost, and schedule baselines. A project plan may be summary or detailed. The PM creates the project management plan based on inputs from the project team and key stakeholders, so it should be agreed upon and approved by the project team and key stakeholders.

Sometimes, people use the term "project plan" to describe the project schedule, Gantt chart, or other document that shows project activities along a timeline. This is incorrect. The project schedule is not the project plan. These types of documents are more accurately described as project schedules and are only one component of a project plan. The PM should be careful to make a distinction between the two when discussing any of these documents with the team, management, or customers because people often reference them incorrectly. MS Project and some other scheduling tools have features beyond project schedule management; one can track cost and create many kinds of reports out of the MS Project. So, people invariably refer to MS Project as the project plan, which is misleading. Make sure that people are talking about the same thing in the discussions. The purpose of the project management plan is to compile a series of management plans to guide the project manager, team members, and customers through the management and controlling of the project.

A project plan typically covers plans for scope management, schedule management, cost management, quality management, resource management for resources such as people, tools, and materials, communications management, project change management, risk management, procurement management, etc. It covers all the nine knowledge areas of project management. These plans can be part of a single document, or the project plan can have references and links to these separate plan documents. This is the reason it is also called an *integrated project plan*. If the contents are documented in separate documents, then care should be taken to avoid duplication of any content or process. Duplication will cause difficulty in maintaining the plan and this may lead to confusion. Content and format may vary a little bit from one organization to other. Some organizations create a Web-based project plan instead of a single document or a series of interlinked documents. These Web applications provide links or menus to different sections of the project plan. If you need to add or update the risk section, then you just need to update that section of the Web page. And when you save the document/Web page, you will be prompted to also update the revision history of the project plan, including the version number, so that a log is created along with a version number. The website is designed in such a way that any time a new version is created, an automatic email goes out to all the important stakeholders, including team members, informing them about the changes made to the plan. This automation makes the life of a project manager easy and prevents the communication breakdown as human intervention is avoided by automatic email generation. Updates to certain sections of the project might lead to the trigger of an email requesting approval of the project plan. This email can go to designated authorities who need to access the website and approve the plan in order to make the revision official. Web administrators are assigned to manage the configuration control part of the website in a way that only the project manager, assistant/deputy project manager, and the administrative support of the PM are given the edit rights to the project plan. Others just have the read access. The project plan document can be downloaded into a Word document for easy review and storage of physical copies.

One of the valuable aspects of the project management plan is the inclusion of project strategies. These strategies are the information concerning the following:

1. *Purpose, scope (in scope and out of scope), and objectives:* This information can be captured from the project charter and SOW at the beginning of the project. Later on, when the scope is detailed, this can be referenced to the scope document.

2. *Assumptions and constraints:* Assumptions are the factors that are considered true, certain, or real for the planning purposes. The assumptions may also be recorded as risks because in case the assumptions turn out to be incorrect, they impact the project positively or negatively. Constraints are the factors that limit the abilities of the project team, such as a hard end date for the project, unskilled human resources, limited budget, stringent quality standards, etc.

3. *Dependencies:* The PM should properly record all the dependencies for the project or any part of the project.

4. *Team organization:* Project organization should be prepared in the beginning and then updated regularly whenever there is any change in the organization.

5. *Roles and responsibilities:* The PM should explicitly record the roles and responsibilities for carrying out the work of the project. This will initiate the need for skill sets required for the project work.

6. *Key contacts:* In general, for big projects a project team roster is prepared that details the names of all team members, customers, and other stakeholders, their contact numbers, email addresses, location, etc.

7. *Project management and control structure, including project governance:* The use of organizational charts or diagrams is recommended to depict the project team's interaction with external entities. This also provides information about the escalation process.

8. *Project tailoring approach:* Not all standard organizational processes apply to every single project. Sometimes, depending on the need of the project, the process must be tailored either to add extra processes or to drop some processes fully or partially. The process tailoring needs should be documented and approved for the project.

9. *List of deliverables, owners, and signoff authorities:* This is explained in more detail later in this book.

10. *Estimation rationale:* Document the tools, methods, assumptions, and processes involved in the estimation process for the deliverables of the project. The PM can avoid a lot of conflits by documenting and communicating the estimation rationale to all key project stakeholders. Schedule and cost are the main areas of conflict.

11. *Success criteria for the proje*ct: Obtain and list all the *critical success factors* (CSFs) for the project. These are the parameters on which the success of the project will be measured. Some example CSFs are that the project must finish by 12/31/2009, final products must pass the quality standards set by the customer, budget should not deviate more than 15 percent at any milestone of the project, etc. This is also called acceptance criteria.

Contrary to common belief, planning does not always finish before execution starts. In fact, planning continues throughout the project to account for the new risks and issues, changes to originally documented assumptions, and to respond to any other unplanned situations. In general, projects exercise rolling wave planning and progressive elaboration. *Rolling wave planning* is the process of planning for a project in waves as the project unfolds. *Progressive elaboration* means that over time, the work packages are elaborated in greater detail. In this approach, immediate future tasks/phases are planned in detail and the remaining future tasks/phases are planned on a high level. So, the project plan is a living document; and as the project evolves, the project plan must be updated continuously. However, every change in the project plan or any supporting plan should be version controlled and should be reviewed and approved by the project team and key stakeholders.

The project plan is vital for any project, irrespective of the size, type, and/or industry. This guides the team through various situations. When a management situation arises, the project plan describes in detail the process that will be used to handle the situation. The PM is the owner of the project plan, but team members and other stakeholders contribute to it. So, make sure that as a project manager, you have the buy-in from all the stakeholders; otherwise it might lead to chaos, conflict, and confusion. Some parts or sections of the plan can be delegated, but ensure that you review those parts and understand them fully as you, the PM, are the owner of this deliverable. For example, you can delegate the Quality Management section to the QA (Quality Assurance) lead of the organization. As mentioned, the PM is responsible for creating and maintaining the project management plan throughout the life of the project. Project managers also become one of the main users of the document and they rely on it quite heavily to help them manage the project. Customers and team members will use the project plan, but mainly as a guide to understand how a process should work. The artifact guides anyone related to the project to understand how the processes and procedures are executed in each of the nine knowledge areas of the project, such as schedule management, cost management, human resource management, quality management, risk management, change management, etc.

Scope Management Plan

Scope is one of the three main pillars of the project. But how is the scope defined? Is it a description of the final product and how the final products and services of the project appear to be? The answer is NO. This is the myopic view of the scope. Scope has two parts: product scope and project scope. Product scope is obvious to everyone; it is defined as the features, properties, and characteristics of the final product and service that the project produces. Project scope, the other hand, refers to the work that needs to be performed in the project to deliver the product, services, and final result. This includes the project management plan, specification document, WBS, schedule, design document, quality testing results, various kinds of project reports as required by the stakeholders, etc.

The scope management plan describes the process and procedure to define, document, verify, manage, and control the scope of the project. This plan should explain in detail how the scope of the project can be defined, roles and responsibilities, process of scope verification, and how the scope will be managed, including the document control process and the change control process. Scope control is very important and a loose process may derail the project beyond repair. So, the plan should illustrate the scope change control process, explaining how the change can be controlled, identified, requested, reviewed, and approved/rejected, and finally how it can become a part of the scope of the project. Because scope definition takes place early in the project, the PM must ensure that the scope management plan is ready as soon as possible and then it is communicated properly to the team members and the customers. This will prevent surprises as well as the concerns that the stakeholders may have later on. In general, the project scope management plan should contain the following:

1. *Project overview:* This comes from the project overview as documented in the project charter or the preliminary project scope document.
2. *Project objectives:* Objectives can also be obtained from the project charter or from the preliminary project scope document.
3. *Scope planning:* This section defines the process to prepare a detailed project scope based on the preliminary project scope document.
4. *Work breakdown structure (WBS):* Describe in detail how the project team can create, maintain, and control the work breakdown structure for the project. WBS is explained in great detail in the next chapter.
5. *Scope verification and approval:* Specify the process for the review, verification, and approval of the scope artifacts. Different deliverables can have different review and approval processes. For example, if the architectural design of the product is complex, then the design document may be group reviewed instead of the general practice of peer review. The RACI matrix as defined later in this book may come in handy for this purpose. The scope verification and approval process from the customer side may take longer than expected and can result in the delay of subsequent tasks and an impact on project schedule. To avoid this situation, establish a time frame, in terms of duration, in consultation with the customer and other stakeholders by making them cognizant of the consequences. The commitment will save a lot of time for the PM in terms of follow-ups and issue resolution.
6. *Scope control:* This process is linked to the change management process of the project. Identify the roles and responsibilities and describe a process for change identification, change request documentation, change request submission, change review, and approval for the scope of the project. Specify the timelines within which the Change Control Board should respond to the request.

The scope management plan includes the tools and techniques used by the project team to follow the above processes. Example of tools and techniques for the scope management process include product analysis, templates, forms, guidelines, standards, alternative identification, analysis tools, configuration management system (such as Visual Source Safe and other document control tools), etc. The tools required for various activities of scope management should be documented in the plan corresponding to the respective activity.

Schedule Management Plan

Schedule management falls under the time management knowledge area of project management. Scope, schedule, and cost are called the triple constraints of the project. So, time management is one of the main areas with which a project manager should be very well versed. The schedule is responsible for most of the conflicts on any project, so time management should be one of the top priorities for a PM. The schedule management plan is part of the project management plan. The project schedule is a deliverable owned by the PM and is different from the schedule management plan and the project management plan. *The project schedule is not a project plan.*

The schedule management plan describes in detail how the schedule will be developed, updated, controlled, and managed. The schedule management plan is not the schedule in itself; rather it is the documentation of the processes and procedures to carry out the schedule management activities. It serves as a guideline for the project manager, project team, and the customers, and defines tools and techniques for development of the schedule, frequency of update, schedule reporting process, how the change in the originally established schedule will be managed and controlled, roles and responsibilities, etc. Change to the baseline schedule is part of the change control process. In general, the schedule management plan should contain details regarding the following:

1. *Tasks and activities:* Explain how the activities and tasks will be identified to produce different project deliverables. The project work breakdown structure (WBS) is generally used to identify the tasks and activities along with their dependencies for scheduling purposes. The project schedule from a similar past project can be used to identify all the tasks required for incorporation into the project schedule.
2. *Estimation:* Once all the tasks are identified and their dependencies established, then the PM would need estimates from the project team, for all the tasks, to develop the schedule. Estimation is done for the effort required to carry out various tasks, which is also an input for cost estimation. Depending on the dependencies and the number of resources available for various tasks, one arrives at the duration. The PM can allocate some buffer for the duration based on the past experience. Other considerations for the duration are the dependencies and hard deadlines. If you have a hard deadline for the project, then divide the respective activity efforts by the allocated duration; this will give you the number of resources required to carry out the task within the given duration. Sometimes it may not be possible and efficient to engage so

many resources on a given task as the above calculation suggests. You might often hear people saying, "Nine moms cannot produce a child in one month." So, in such cases, look for the work-around to finish the task in the required duration. At the same time document this as a risk and discuss with upper management and the customers.

3. *Schedule development:* The schedule management plan should define the tools, roles and responsibilities, and the process for schedule development, as well as subsequent updates to the schedule. Standard tools available in the marketplace (e.g., MS Project, Planview, etc.) perform this job once the task details, resource details, effort/duration, and dependencies are input into the tool. MS Project is the most common tool used industrywide.

4. *Schedule control:* Changes are inevitable in projects, and no matter how much attention you pay, schedule changes might be necessary in the project owing to multiple reasons. This section of the plan defines the process to initiate and execute the change control related to schedule. This is linked to the change management plan of the project.

5. *Reporting:* Identify and describe the details regarding how and when the project schedule information will be reported to team members, senior management, and the customers.

In general, organizations have a standard template for scheduling, which mostly serves both as a WBS and a schedule template. There are many scheduling tools available in the marketplace that make the job of a project manager easy. For example, MS Project has features that draw network diagrams, calculate critical paths of the project, draw Gantt charts, provide information about resource usage (so that you can do the resource leveling), etc. Apart from this, you can mark a particular task as a milestone task, assign predecessors and successors, baseline project tasks, and produce various kinds of reports, etc.

Initially, when a project starts, the PMs do not have a lot of detailed information, so they cannot prepare the detailed schedule. Senior management, customers, and the project team should not expect a detailed schedule at this point. At this time, the project may have a milestone schedule, showing the start and end dates of summary or the major milestone tasks. These milestone dates will be the tentative dates based on the ballpark estimate (OOM estimate) available in the beginning of the project. Sometimes the end date can be a fixed date because of regulatory requirements, product launch date, or some other constraints (e.g., Y2K). Once the requirements analysis is complete and the project team understands the project scope well, then the team can be asked to provide effort estimates broken down for major activities, resource availabilities, resource constraints, and assumptions made during the estimation. Based on these inputs and considering other constraints, the PM should come up with a detailed schedule for the project. The timelines should be discussed with team members, scheduling conflicts should be resolved, and finally when the team approves of the schedule, it should be baselined and communicated and discussed with senior management and the customer. Note that cost estimates and schedule estimates go hand in hand. At this point in time, the schedule and budget are locked down with a high degree of confidence. If the originally established project end date remains the same, then the PM need not do anything even if the interim milestone dates differ. If the final date is beyond the originally expected end date, the PM should initiate a change request for the change in schedule. Until the change request is approved, the project implementation date should not be changed and the project should be reported in yellow status even if everything else is in green. Once the change request is approved, the end date should be changed to the new date and the project can be brought to green status considering that everything else is green. If the PMs do not understand this concept well, they will always face difficulty managing the stakeholders' expectations regarding project time management. The project schedule should be baselined once in the beginning of the project even though the details are not available. It should be re-baselined once the schedule is locked down and every time it goes through the change control approval process as described above.

The dependency among the work effort, resource unit, and the duration was discussed briefly above. However, it is very important to understand this concept in general and how MS Project utilizes this concept to deliver the schedule.

$$\text{Work Effort/Resource Unit} = \text{Duration}$$

or

$$\text{Work Effort} = \text{Duration} \times \text{Resource Unit}$$

Suppose a task is estimated to take eighty hours (work effort, or simply called "work" = 80 hr) for a particular skilled worker to finish. If we deploy two such skilled workers (Resource Unit = 2), then the work can be done in one working week (Duration = 1 week). Here, it is assumed that each worker works for eight hours a day and there are five working days in a week. As shown in Figure 2.2, if you double-click on any particular task in MS Project, the task information window is displayed. Go to the "Advanced" tab and then look at the options in the drop-down list for the "Task type." You will find three options: "Fixed Duration," "Fixed Units," and "Fixed Work." Depending on the situation, you can make one of these factors fixed. For that task, if you manually fix the value of any one of the other two variables, then MS Project will adjust the value of the third factor by itself to come up with the schedule. There is one more option; you can make the schedule dependent on the effort by checking the box "Effort driven." The "Effort driven" option should be chosen when the resource allocation is fixed and you want to find out the amount of effort required for a given period. Suppose you want to get a particular task finished in ten days; you should set the "Task type" to "Fixed Duration." Now if you have two people working full-time on the task and you make the task effort driven, then the "Work" column in MS Project will show a total value of 160 hours. You can go to the "Resources" tab on the "Task Information" toolbar and change

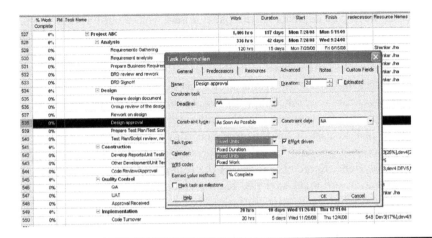

	% Work Complete	PM	Task Name	Work	Duration	Start	Finish	redecessor	Resource Names
527	0%		⊟ Project ABC	1,406 hrs	197 days	Mon 7/28/08	Mon 5/11/09		
528	0%		⊟ Analysis	336 hrs	42 days	Mon 7/28/08	Wed 9/24/08		
529	0%		Requirements Gathering	120 hrs	15 days	Mon 7/28/08	Fri 8/15/08		Shankar Jha
530	0%		Requirement analysis						nkar Jha
531	0%		Prepare Business Requirem						nkar Jha
532	0%		BRD review and rework						nkar Jha
533	0%		BRD Signoff						nkar Jha
534	0%		⊟ Design						
535	0%		Prepare design document						
536	0%		Group review of the design						
537	0%		Rework on design						
538	0%		Design approval						
539	0%		Prepare Test Plan/Test Scr						
540	0%		Test Plan/Script review, rev						
541	0%		⊟ Construction						
542	0%		Develop Reports/Unit Testi						3[25%],dev4[2
543	0%		Other Development/Unit Te						5
544	0%		Code Review/Approval						3,dev4 DEV5,/
545	0%		⊟ Quality Control						
546	0%		QA						
547	0%		UAT						nkar Jha
548	0%		Approval Received						
549	0%		⊟ Implementation	20 hrs	10 days	Wed 11/26/08	Thu 12/11/08		
550	0%		Code Turnover	20 hrs	5 days	Wed 11/26/08	Thu 12/4/08	548	Dev3[17%],dev4[1

Task Information dialog box overlay:

General | Predecessors | Resources | Advanced | Notes | Custom Fields

Name: Design approval   Duration: 2d   ☐ Estimated

Constrain task
Deadline: NA

Constraint type: As Soon As Possible   Constraint date: NA

Task type: Fixed Units   ☑ Effort driven
(Fixed Duration / Fixed Units / Fixed Work)
Calendar:
WBS code:

Earned value method: % Complete
☐ Mark task as milestone

Help   OK   Cancel

Figure 2.2   Use of task type in project schedule.

the "Resource Unit." Suppose you keep one resource 100 percent and change the allocation for the other resource to 50 percent, then the "Work" field will change to 120 hours. What happens if you uncheck the "Effort driven" field for the task? If you have unchecked this field and have the duration set as fixed, you can change the "Work" value manually to any value; the duration, will not change (because you have already fixed it) but the Resource Unit will change to balance the equation above. Similarly, if you keep the "Work" fixed (in the task type field on task information) and manually change the duration, then the Resource Unit will also be adjusted. Summarizing the concept: if you keep one of the three values constant and you manually change the value of the second field, the third will be adjusted automatically in order to balance the above equation. In general, all scheduling tools work on this fundamental concept.

The Gantt chart, one of the important schedule communication tools, along with some other schedule communication tools are explained in detail in Chapter 3. Whether the schedule is prepared with the help of an elaborate tool, using MS Excel, using some kind of drawing, or is prepared on a sheet of paper, every schedule should, at the very least, include major tasks, start and finish dates, duration, percent completion, and the resources working on the tasks. This is one of the very important communication tools for project managers. It would be an understatement if we call the schedule *the mother of all reports* in a project. At the same time, the genesis of the schedule lies in consideration of all aspects of the project, may it be resource, scope, effort (which in turn is cost), quality, risk, issue, change, process, methodology, etc. So, *schedule is all-encompassing.* This fact emphasizes the importance of the schedule in project communication; hence, PMs pay a great deal of attention to the preparation, updating, and reporting of schedule. Schedule preparation could be easy and simple for small projects and could be very time consuming and complex for big and complex projects.

Whether simple or complex in the background, you should always produce a simple view to the team members and stakeholders so that they can understand easily and clearly. The main project schedule could be very huge and complex, but the PM should use various tools to extract the portion of the main schedule to present a simple view to various audiences, depending on the circumstances. You cannot throw your schedule with a thousand tasks to every audience. Some stakeholders may be interested in the milestone schedule while others may be interested in that part of the schedule that is owned by a particular functional area. Sometimes you may be asked to present a detailed schedule to get particular work done. Remember that it is the responsibility of the PM to facilitate communication and make sure that team members and stakeholders understand the project schedule well. Any confusion may cost you dearly. The next chapter (Chapter 3) explains some smart ways of communicating the schedule to different audiences under different circumstances.

Cost Management Plan

Cost is the third constituent of the triple constraint of a project. Cost management should not be confused with business financial management. Project cost management is a specialized knowledge area, different from financial management discipline. Customers and project owners are very strict with the project budget these days, so it is essential that the project has a well-defined plan for cost estimation, budgeting, and control. The cost management plan explains the processes involved in planning, estimating, budgeting, and controlling costs so that the project can be completed within the approved budget. Cost planning is linked to human resource planning and schedule planning. Cost estimation serves as input to the project schedule. At the same time, the budget takes input from the project schedule. Cost control is directly linked to the change management process.

The cost management plan should include processes for the following:

1. *Cost estimation:* Cost estimates are refined during the course of the project to reflect the additional details available. The project could have a rough order of magnitude (ROM) estimate in the range of –50 to +100 percent in the initial phase of the project. Later, as more details are known, estimates could narrow down to a range of –10 to +15 percent. Refinement and estimation accuracy increase as the project progresses. The project, by its very nature, is elaborated progressively because all the details are not known in the beginning. Scope, cost, and schedule estimation follow the principle of progressive elaboration. Once the WBS for the project is complete, effort and other resource (material, service, capital, etc., if applicable to the project) estimates are made for every work package in the WBS.

The resource rate is applied, corresponding to the effort and other unit of estimation that give the cost of individual work activity in the WBS. When summed, one arrives at the total cost of the project. Assumptions made during the estimation process should be recorded and discussed within the team. Some of these assumptions may go to the risk register. In general, organizations have estimator tools that can be tailored for the purpose of the specific projects. The cost management plan explicitly recognizes the frequency and check points when the estimations need to be refined, the tolerance percentage at every stage, and the review and signoff authorities involved during these stages in case the change exceeds the tolerance limit. Roles and responsibilities for estimations at various phases of the project might vary because the project team expands and shrinks as the project moves along.

Data from similar past project can be considered during the estimation process, but the person doing the estimations must consider the strengths and weaknesses of the human resources doing the actual work for the project. This is called *analogous estimation.* Suggestions should be taken from the experts of the subject matter. When the team understands the project well and has done sufficient analysis, the PM should ask the functional managers or the functional leads working on the project to come up with the estimates. The PMs should not do the estimation themselves. Once the functional groups present their estimate, the PM should then discuss, review, and understand the logic and notion behind their estimates and, if needed, the estimate should be revised.

2. *Cost budgeting:* Budgeting the project cost is required to establish a baseline against which the project cost performance measurement can be done. In simple language, costs of individual schedule activities are aggregated to come up with a baseline for every milestone. For the purpose of performance measurement, the actual cost of the project at certain milestones can be compared against the budget/baseline established for the project at that milestone. For example, a project has a budget of $0.5 MN at the end of Analysis, $1.0 MN at the end of Design (Analysis + Design), $2.0 MN at the end of Construction (Analysis + Design + Construction), $2.5 MN at the end of Quality Testing, and $3.0 MN at the end of the project. An S curve is generally used to report the cost performance, along with the schedule and scope of the project. The S curve is described in detail in Chapter 3. Sometimes, the sponsor might impose a funding limit for the project. Under this arrangement, only the budgeted amount of funds is disbursed to the project for every milestone. This is done to regulate project spending so that it goes along with the completion of the project scope as established during project budgeting. This process is called *funding limit reconciliation.* Management can keep some reserve for the project as a cost buffer, which can be used in case of eventualities.

3. *Cost control:* This process is directly attached to the change management process of the project. The plan should document how the root cause responsible for affecting changes to the cost baseline can be identified and eliminated, the process of initiating the change control, templates and tools need to be used for requesting the change, the process of change review and approval, and finally how the baseline changes can be incorporated into the project and reported to the stakeholders. Change can be both positive and negative. In case the locked-down cost is not supposed to deviate below, say –10 percent and if the project manager is convinced that the actual cost will be less than –10 percent of the budget, then he/she should initiate a change control.

4. *Cost reporting:* The project cost management plan should identify the reporting needs, frequency, format, tool, roles, and responsibilities. If the sponsor has not asked for any particular frequency, then cost and budget summary information should be incorporated into the project status report on a weekly basis. Apart from this, cost performance should be reported in the milestone report, phase gate review report, as well as at project closure.

There are several ways to maintain and track project cost. Some organizations and project managers use simple MS Excel spreadsheets as a cost tracker, while others use big and elaborate tools. Figure 2.3 provides an example of a simple cost tracker.

The Earned Value Technique (EVT) is an elaborate and common cost reporting tool. The analysis performed using earned value is called the Earned Value Analysis (EVA). EVA is used for reporting cost, schedule, and scope performance together, and it is a powerful reporting tool. Understanding the terms defined below will help in performing an EVA. MS Project and some other tools have features that provide the EVA. For the purpose of explaining this concept, suppose a project started in January and you are measuring the progress at the end of three months in the beginning of April. Assume that the analysis phase of the project was supposed to finish by the end of March.

■ *Planned Value (PV):* The budgeted cost (baseline cost) for the amount of work supposed to finish at a given point in time. In the example above, the PV for the analysis phase (at the end of March) would be $155,000.

■ *Earned Value (EV):* The budgeted cost of the actual work that finished at a given point in time. In the example, let's assume that only 80 percent of the analysis could be completed by the end of March. So, the EV at the end of March will be $0.8 \times \$155,000 = \$124,000$.

■ *Actual Cost (AC):* This is very straightforward; AC is the actual cost incurred by the project at a given point in time, starting from the beginning of the project. In the above example, AC = $39,240 + $54,000 + $65,700 = $158,940.

■ *Cost Variance (CV)* = EV − AC = −$34,940.

■ *Schedule Variance (SV)* = EV − PV = −$31,000.

■ *Cost Performance Index (CPI)* = EV/AC = 0.78.

	Jan	Feb	Mar	Apr	May	June
Monthly Budget	$45,000	$50,000	$60,000	$65,000	$65,000	$70,000
Cumulative Budget	$45,000	$95,000	$155,000	$220,000	$285,000	$355,000
Actual Effort per Resource						
A	160	160	50			
B	40	120	160			
C	40	80	160			
D	20	40	100			
E	80	80	120			
F	96	120	140			
Total Actual Effort	436	600	730	0	0	0
Actual Cost (Effort × Rate)	$39,240	$54,000	$65,700	$0	$0	$0
Cumulative Actual Cost	$39,240	$93,240	$158,940			
Cost Variance	$5,760	($4,000)	($5,700)			

Figure 2.3 Simple cost tracker.

- *Schedule Performance Index (SPI)* = EV/PV = 0.8.
- *Budget at Completion (BAC):* Total budget at the end of the project, which is nothing but the PV at the end of the project. Assuming that June is the end of the project, then BAC = \$355,000.
- *Estimate to Complete (ETC):* As the name suggests, ETC is the cost of the work remaining to be done to finish the project. If the current trend continues, then ETC = (BAC − EV)/CPI. In case something is done to make up for the slippage, or if the project team forecasts that future performance will be worse, then the ETC will be equal to the new estimates for the entire remaining work.
- *Estimate at Complete (EAC):* EAC is the total cost at the end of the project. EAC = AC + ETC.

The ETC and EAC are used for the forecasting purposes. When PV, EV, and AC are plotted against time, they produce an S curve, which is a very powerful tool. The S curve is described in detail in Chapter 3.

Human Resource (HR) Management Plan

As per the PMI, human resource planning determines project roles, responsibilities, and reporting relationships, and creates the staffing management plan. The human resource plan addresses the human resource needs to accomplish the project objectives. The staffing plan, which is part of the human resource plan, contains details about how and when project team members will be acquired, the criteria of releasing them from the project, the identification of training needs, plans for rewards and recognition, compliance considerations, safety issues, and the impact of the staff management plan on the organization. The main contents of the HR plan include:

1. Responsibility assignment matrix (RAM)
2. Roles and responsibilities
3. Project organization chart
4. Staffing management plan

The RAM, roles and responsibilities, and organization chart are discussed in detail later in this book.

The purpose of a human resource plan is to capture and document the project staffing requirements. First of all, assess the nature of the work required to deliver the products and services. Based on the type of work, capture inputs about the functional skills required to work on all kinds of deliverables of the project. Use the information to map deliverables against resources to prepare the RAM. Next, identify the roles and responsibilities for the project. Prepare an organization chart that encompasses the project team, project governing body, customer organization involved in the project, vendor organization involved in the project, organization of other units or applications that might have dependencies on the project, etc. The staffing management plan has information about how, when, what, and how much staff will be acquired and released. Obtain the resource names from the respective resource managers for each of the roles and get a commitment that resources will be ramped up and ramped down as per the staffing plan. The HR plan should be updated as per the needs and changes to the project and appropriate resources should be acquired, trained, and released with the help of resource managers. The success of the project depends on the kind of resources available to the project. So, work very closely with the functional/resource manager and in the case that resource issues are not resolved by the resource manager, escalate through proper communication channels so that executives are aware of the risks and issues and can take appropriate action. The cost and schedule plan should be updated based on the resource availability to the project.

The HR plan also contains details about how the HR plan will be executed and how the resource situation will be managed and controlled. The use of resource histograms is very common for planning, executing, monitoring, and controlling human resources. MS Project and MS Excel are other tools used for this purpose. The HR plan is very closely associated with the cost management plan. Resource fluctuations affect the burn rate and finally the project cost. Keep a constant watch on the progress of the project and assess the future resource requirements accordingly. Sometimes, different members on the project have different billing rates; in such situations, you should be sensitive to the usage of costlier resources in comparison to not so costly resources. HR planning and execution is a very time-consuming exercise, and the PM must constantly keep watch over the situation and upgrade the plan regularly (in most cases, weekly). Any changes in the scope, schedule, budget, or quality of the project may have an impact on the current resource requirements and resource forecasts for the future.

Apart from human resources, the project manager should also prepare a plan for other types of resources, such as machine, material, hardware, software, tool, etc. required to execute the project.

Communication Management Plan

The project communication management plan describes processes to ensure timely and appropriate generation, collection, dissemination, storage, and disposal of project information. As per the PMI, this document explains how the communication needs and expectations for the project will be met, how and in what format information will be communicated, when and where each communication will be made, and who is responsible for each type of communication. A communication management plan can be formal or informal, highly detailed or broadly framed, and is based on the requirements of the project stakeholders. The communication management plan provides:

1. Stakeholder communication requirements
2. Information to be communicated, including format, content, and level of detail
3. Person responsible for communicating the information
4. Person or groups who will receive the information
5. Methods or technologies used to convey the information, such as memoranda, email, and/or press releases
6. Frequency of the communication, such as weekly, monthly, etc.
7. Escalation process: identifying time frames and the management chain (names) for escalation of issues that cannot be resolved at a lower staff level
8. Method for updating and refining the communications management plan as the project progresses and develops
9. Glossary of common terminology

The communication matrix, discussed later in this book, is a good summary of some of the items discussed above. The communication management plan can also include guidelines for project status meetings, project team meetings, e-meetings, and emails. The plan should identify all kinds of reports, along with their frequency, to be prepared and distributed in the project. Cover the communication requirements of the stakeholders while addressing all communication issues that may occur in the project. Historical information from past projects and organizational process assets should be referred to before creating the communication management plan. Communication planning requires inputs from the customers for their communication requirements. Understand what reports, documents, deliverables, and forms the customers need. Inquire and confirm the template, format, and frequency for every communication, as well as the recipients of these communications. Project managers generally ignore these details in the beginning of the project because the lack of these details in the plan may not impact the project immediately. However, these small things matter a lot in the long run.

Overall, this part of the project plan describes all aspects of the management of project communication. It documents the procedures that the PM and the team members will follow to gather, create, and distribute the project information. Because communication plays a vital role in the success of any project, one must consider devoting enough time for the planning and then managing of the communication throughout the project. The PM spends most of his/her time in communication. However, he/she is responsible for the effectiveness and efficiency of not only his/her communication, but also for all communication happening in the entire project. The PM must lay out a protocol and must monitor to ensure that team members are following it properly. The project team is formed by bringing together people from different departments and organizations. Many times they have not worked together and sometimes they don't even know each other. People from different organizations must work cohesively to obtain the desired project results. However, there is always friction between different groups and organizations because of their varying interests, internal politics, and also the ways they understand and perceive things. People might pursue their own goals and their activities may not be aligned with the goals of the project. A project demands that all groups coordinate with each other and work together. There is always a dependency between/among the teams in terms of work and information. In such situations, it is essential that they communicate promptly, proactively, properly, and as per the protocol set in the project communication management plan. If a team or an individual is waiting for some information from a different team or individual, then he/she should not depend on the PM to serve as a messenger or the coordinator—unless it is absolutely required. Similarly, the other group or individual should respond appropriately. The PM needs to intervene in cases where there is a breakdown in communication or if the communication is not taking place properly. Remind team members and other stakeholders about their roles in communication and how communication breakdown affects project goals. If the situation does not improve or it is not satisfactory, then gather inputs from them about improving the communication. The PM should try to resolve the communication challenges at his/her level first. Sometimes this may not work as desired; it is imperative in such a case that the project manager escalate the matter through proper channels as defined in the communication management plan.

One of the important jobs of a PM is to watch out for extra and unnecessary communication. Extra communication is hazardous because it reduces the efficiency of team members and causes overhead. For example, senior management need not know every little detail of the work that the team members are carrying out. If you copy them on every email, you might be questioned on every little issue that that team faces on a daily basis, issues that do not need management attention. Such interventions will take your time in explaining things every now and then.

New and junior team members might hesitate to ask questions. The PM and the resource manager should ensure that such members get enough coaching and backup so that deliverables and timelines are not impacted. Make sure these team members understand the method, channel, technology, format, and frequency of the communication very well. This can be achieved if all team members go through the project plan in general, and the communication management plan in particular. Any time a new communication channel, a new communication method, or a new communication technology is introduced in the project, the PM should inform all concerned stakeholders in a timely manner. Make sure that fundamental changes to the communication management plan are approved by the appropriate authorities.

Change Management Plan

The change management plan describes the process of change identification and strategy to respond to the change in a formal manner. There is a saying that "If everything is going exactly to plan, something somewhere is going massively wrong." Changes are inevitable in projects, so they should be formally managed and controlled and that is the reason an appropriate plan is essential. This document is also called a *change control plan*. This plan clearly defines what is considered a change. In general, changes to the baseline of any one or more of the triple constraints (schedule, scope, and cost) are considered a change. Be careful, as most of the time people have a narrow understanding of scope. Scope is not just the requirements specification of the final product—it goes beyond that. Scope is defined in detail in the section entitled "Scope Management Plan." The plan outlines the entire process flow, from change initiation to its closure, and details the input, output, and tools involved. It mentions roles and responsibilities and identifies the names of the people involved in the review and approval of the change request. The change request document is discussed as a separate topic later in this chapter.

Changes often upset people, but as a mature project manager you should expect changes in every project. If you know how to handle the changes, then you will love your job; otherwise, it will become a nightmare. If changes are not identified, controlled, and managed properly, they will derail any project and will create an environment of chaos and confusion in the project. Change should never be discouraged; rather, it should be handled properly. Suppose the customer is asking for a change in scope of the project. Then, as a PM, understand the change; meet with your experts to analyze the impact to the existing scope, time, and budget; and then submit a change request as per the change control plan and incorporate the scope change only after the change request is approved. Until the change request is approved, the project team should continue doing business as usual. In another example, suppose that after a couple of months into the project, you realize that the project will exceed the OOM (Order of Magnitude) budget by more than 100 percent and it will be difficult to meet the timelines. In this case, you should write a change request form to suggest changes in budget and timeline. Be sure you gather enough inputs to predict new cost and times, and ensure that the changes are reasonably justified.

The change management plan, a part of the project management plan, should include the following:

1. *Change Control Board (CCB), roles and responsibilities:* Describes the people who should participate in the change control meetings along with their roles and responsibilities.
2. *Process of the change request:* Incorporates the process flow for the entire change control life cycle, explaining steps involved in change initiation, preparation of the change request document, submission of the request to the

change control board, review and appraisal system, time frames, and finally the approval process.

3. *Change request documentation:* Lists the names of all the documents that need to be created or updated for a single change request. Templates are mentioned for new documents. Some of the documents that need to be updated include the project plan (to update the new scope, budget, and time), contract document, SOW, design, test plan, etc. This section also includes the time frames within which the documents need to be created or updated.

4. *Criteria for approval and denial of the change request:* In most cases, this will not vary from project to project and will follow standard process of the organization.

5. *Additional information*, such as the process for emergency change request, change control information distribution, change control document storage, etc.

Big and complex projects can have too many change requests. This requires proper maintenance of the change request log so that all the information is readily available for tracking purposes. This gives a quick reference of what the original budget and schedule were and how the project has arrived at the new budget and schedule. It also provides details of the scope changes. The change request log contains summary information on all the change requests on a high level. Some organizations have Web-based links that upload the change requests automatically create a log, and the PM does not need to make a separate document. In case such an infrastructure or tool does not exist, you can create a simple MS Excel-based spreadsheet as in Figure 2.4. Even if the change request is denied, it should be recorded. The change request log should be accessible to the project team and to upper management.

Defect Management Plan

The defect management plan is part of the project plan that outlines the process for defining, documenting, managing, and controlling the defects. Managing defects involves the process of initiation, tracking, and finally closure of the defect, which covers the entire defect life cycle. The plan identifies the tool that the project team needs to use for defect management. A user guideline for general usage of the tool and specific guidelines for any tailoring made to the tool for project purposes is also part of this plan. User guidelines, apart from providing instructions on how to use the tool, also explain in detail the user groups defined in the defect management tool. The plan outlines the roles and responsibilities for handling various activities in the defect management process. These roles and responsibilities may be mapped to the user groups. Typical user groups for a software project might be the project manager, developer, business analyst, tester, and administrator (who maintains the

| CR # | Description | Change | | | Date Requested | Status | Date Approved or Denied | Requested by | Comments |
		Scope	Budget	Schedule					
AC-01	Modify the main entrance	Y	$10K	2 weeks	6/1/2008	Approved	6/10/2008	Robert B	
AC-02	Budget change due to high cost of cement	N	$12K	N	7/6/2008	Denied		Shankar Jha	CCB Feedback: Compensate budget by reducing labor cost.
AC-03	Delay due to late arrival of inventory	N	N	4 weeks	11/1/2008	Open		Shankar Jha	

Figure 2.4   Change Request log.

tool and provides users with the privileges to perform certain actions using the tool). Defect tracking might include preparation of the defect matrix, checkpoint meetings, escalation procedures, etc. Most often, this plan is part of the quality management plan, which in turn is a subsidiary of the project management plan.

Figure 2.5 shows a typical defect life cycle in a software life-cycle project, which can vary somewhat from organization to organization and from industry to industry. Terminologies can also vary based on the industry and organization, but the concept remains the same. Various defect status types are defined within braces in the box against each defect status type. The standard defect status types include new, assigned, open, deferred, duplicate, reject, fixed, ready for test, closed, and reopen.

There are tools available in the marketplace (e.g., MQC, Rational ClearQuest) that are very handy in performing the defect management process. They can

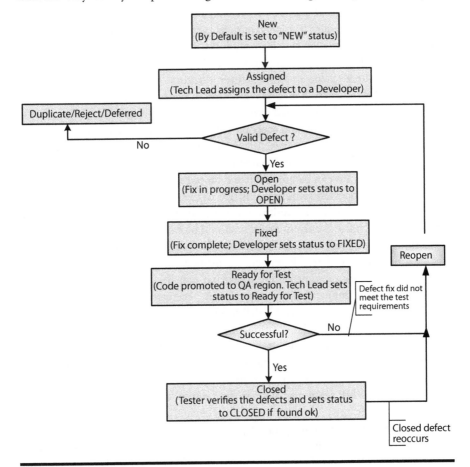

Figure 2.5   Defect life cycle.

produce excellent useful reports for both project managers and quality managers. These reports provide information on the progress of testing and the health of a project based on the percentage of test cases that have been executed, how many have passed, how many critical defects are open, whether or not the testing is on schedule, etc.

Defects are costly to the project, and that is the reason a substantial portion of the project effort goes into the prevention (training, investment in process improvement initiatives, investment in defect prevention tools, etc.) and appraisal (review, verification, validation, testing) of defects and then to the subsequent rework. The indirect costs of defect involve low employee morale, customer dissatisfaction, lost market opportunity for the organization, etc. It is nearly impossible to eliminate defects occurring in the deliverables. We reckon that defects are inevitable; however, they can be minimized by following the right kind of process to identify the defects as early in the life cycle as possible. *Prevention is better than cure.* So, someone has rightly said, "Prepare and prevent; otherwise, repair and repent." So, the primary goal of defect management is to prevent defects from occurring. It is not possible to prevent all detects. The next step is to catch the defect as early as possible and fix it to minimize the impact to the project. Correction is more costly if the defect is not caught at the source whenever and wherever it occurs.

Organizations must establish and maintain a defect management methodology or a framework so that it is integrated into the process of the project. The project should incorporate into its estimates and schedule the task of defect prevention, review, testing, and verification of deliverables. The rigor and extent of these quality assurance/control processes depend on the company policy as well as project-specific need. Sometimes the process can be tailored based on the demand and specific situation of the project. The process to some extent is tied to the risk strategy of the project.

Defect prevention (DP) requires a significant investment from the organization. Data from past and current projects should be captured and analyzed properly after taking inputs from past and present team members and other experts in the organization. Control charts, Pareto charts, fishbone diagrams, brainstorming, and PDCA are examples of some of the tools that can be used to achieve this. This is part of the continuous process improvement exercise, which is a requirement for CMM (Capability Maturity Model) level 5 and some other quality standards. The output may result in the creation of checklists, guideline documents, tools, and identification of training needs. Training may consist of elaborate, full-fledged training or it may be as simple as coaching and mentoring. Defect data from multiple projects may suggest that a lot of design defects of a similar nature repeat in every project. The DP team may suggest the creation of a simple checklist to cover for all the common mistakes thus identified. The quality assurance group can make the use of checklists mandatory in all projects during the creation and review of design documents. Checklists can be updated from time to time based on data analysis by the DP team. Similarly, suppose that during the analysis through the fishbone diagram, the DP team finds that a lot of coding errors in software projects occur due to human oversight, which has been very difficult to eliminate. The DP team may suggest the creation and use of tools for faster turnaround and defect-free code. A quality improvement goal should be set so that it is aligned with the organization-level goal. Defect data should be captured and analyzed regularly to find out the impact of process improvement. Suppose, for one of the programs, on an average that there were five defects found in production per 1000 hours. Defect data was captured and analyzed to find out the root causes, and subsequently process improvements were suggested. Based on the defect data for which process improvement is being implemented, it was decided that a 20-percent improvement could be achieved in three months. Hence, the program should not expect more than four production defects per 1000 hours after three months. Data should be captured after three months and, if there is a large variation compared to the goal, then further analysis should be done to find out why the process improvement did not work. It may also happen that the process improvement worked but the variation was caused by some other factors.

Implementation of the defect management program in any organization needs the full support of senior management. This support is needed in the form of time, resource, and budget commitments. The project team should collect and analyze the data by itself with support from the quality assurance team. To this effect, a DP team should be established and a DP lead should be identified. The DP lead is a person who champions the defect management process in the project. However, a defect management process needs time and input from everyone on the team. These expectations should be documented in the defect management plan and should be communicated to the project team and to all functional managers.

Quality Management Plan

What is quality? We use the term very often in our day-to-day lives. Different pundits have defined the term in many ways. Quality is defined from two different perspectives: from a producer's view and from a customer's view.

- Philip Crosby: Quality is *conformance to requirements*. He defines quality from a producer's perspective, but requirements may not fully represent customer expectations.
- Juran Joseph: Quality is *fitness for use*. Fitness is defined by the customer.
- Peter Drucker: Quality in a product or service is not what the supplier puts in. It is what the customer gets out and is willing to pay for.

Apart from this, some organizations and quality frameworks have also defined quality in their own way. Six Sigma defines quality as the number of defects per million opportunities. As per ISO 9000, it is the degree to which a set of inherent characteristics fulfills requirements.

You may have come across the terms "small q" and "big Q." Organizations implement quality at various levels based on their maturity. When the scope of quality is restricted to a small team, certain products, certain deliverables, and focuses on issues related to a few projects or departments, then it is called small q (meaning small quality); it is also called *little q*. Big Q is vast in scope. When cross-functional groups and large teams are involved in identifying and coming up with solutions to problems across the organization, it is termed as big Q.

According to the PMI, the quality management plan describes how the project management team implements the performing organization's quality policy. The quality management plan provides input to the overall project management plan and must address the following:

1. Quality management approach
2. Quality control (QC) procedure
3. Quality assurance (QA) procedure
4. Continuous process improvement plan for the project
5. Roles and responsibilities
6. Quality tools to be used by the project team (e.g., Pareto chart, brainstorming, control chart, etc.)
7. Quality matrix

Details regarding the approach for review, inspection, verification, validation, testing, and audit are described in this plan. A quality baseline and the goals for various quality parameters are determined up-front and documented in the plan. It documents the groups and individuals from inside and outside the project team who should be involved in the QC, QA, and process improvement activities. These are essentially the roles and responsibilities for carrying out the quality process. The plan also captures information about the tools that the project will be using. It is important to understand the difference between quality control and quality assurance. *Quality control* is an activity that verifies whether or not the product produced meets standards. It relates to and is concerned with a specific product or service. Quality control verifies whether specific attribute(s) are in or not in a specific product or service. *Quality assurance* would measure the process to find weaknesses in the process and then correct those weaknesses to continually (there is a difference between continual and continuous improvement) improve the process. Quality assurance evaluates whether or not quality control is working for the primary purpose of determining whether or not there is a weakness in the process. Quality assurance is always called quality control over quality control because it evaluates whether quality control is working. Quality assurance is concerned with all the products that will ever be produced by a process. QC is a staff function whereas QA is a line function.

With the growing global competition among companies, there is more and more emphasis on quality. Quality cannot just be controlled or managed at the final stage or in the final products and services. The concept and practice of quality must be incorporated starting from the initiation of the project through to the closure of the project at each and every stage. For example, the requirements document and design document are not the final products, but still they need to go through the quality control process. The organization may have processes for sampling, verification, validation, review, and testing of each and every deliverable. The deliverable may be an interim product or the final product, depending on the type of deliverable. The project follows those processes. The quality management plan portion of the project plan details how these processes should be followed, the person(s) or group responsible, the signing authorities, the sequence of processes, and the level of control required for the specific project. The processes must be further elaborated to suit the project, and the plan defines in detail the types of testing (unit, integration, regression, independent, etc.); types of review (peer review, group review, independent review, customer review, etc.); types of sampling; and types of audit, etc. that the project will follow. Sometimes the project may need to deviate from the process of the organization; such deviations should be documented by the PM and authorized by the quality assurance department of the organization. If there is no formal quality assurance unit, the project governing board should authorize such process tailoring. These deviations may be due to various reasons—customers may demand more stringent quality control than the organization has in place, the timeline and/or budget of the project may not allow full practice of quality assurance and quality control, an unskilled workforce may require more review and testing of the products, etc. Some projects have time constraints; for example, an insurance plan is to be launched in the market in the beginning of next year, which is just six months away. The new plan requires software to enroll the new members and to process their claims. If the software project follows all the required quality processes, the project will not be completed on time and the company will lose tremendous amounts of money and market credibility. Hence, the CIO of the company wants the basic infrastructure to be built so that the new business can be supported even though the software may not be efficient and may require more work later on.

In general, the quality management plan describes steps that should be taken by the project team to ensure that the product or service generated out of the project will meet the stakeholders' expectations. Depending on the standard of the organization and the quality requirements of the customer, the project plan defines a quality matrix for the project. The quality matrix is described in detail along with examples later in this book.

Quality management is always perceived as an overhead and thus is often overlooked. However, if the quality practices are established and followed properly, then it pays rich dividends, saves a lot of time and effort for the organization, and results in higher customer satisfaction, higher employee satisfaction, and higher employee morale. The lack of a quality management plan can lead to lower attention paid to quality on the part of the employees. In most cases, the PM has to take the lead in preparing the plan and then communicating that plan to the customer and to project team members. However, in some organizations, someone from the quality assurance department takes the lead.

Risk Management Plan

This is the document that describes how risk management will be structured and performed on the project. Its purpose is to document the process and procedures for managing all kinds of project risks. Information contained in the risk management plan varies by application area and project size. Note that the risk management plan is different from the risk register. The former is broader in scope than the latter, which contains the list of project risks, the result of risk analysis, and the risk responses. A project, by its very nature, contains risk no matter how small or big it is. This point should be very clear to the PM and to senior management. One of the biggest challenges on a project is managing risk. For this reason, it is very important that the project establishes a set of processes and procedures to deal with risk. It is quite difficult to handle risks properly without having a set of processes and guidelines.

Before moving forward, let us understand what a risk is and how it is different from an issue. In simple language, *risk is an uncertain event.* It is a risk until the event has not occurred. When the event occurs, it can have a positive (called opportunity) or a negative (called threat) impact on at least one objective of the project. Once the event takes place and if that event has a negative impact, then it is called an issue. Therefore, risk is a future event, which may or may not happen. Risk can have good as well as bad results, but issues are always associated with a problem. Issue is a current problem that needs to be fixed. Risk is always uncertain and so it has a probability assigned to it. If the risk has positive impact then the project manager should plan for such action that maximizes the impact. At the same time, if the risk has a negative impact then the project manager should plan for minimizing or eliminating the impact based on the risk tolerance capabilities of the customer and the senior management.

Risk management is a very important aspect of project management. Organizations running projects should have strong processes in place to deal with the risks and issues. Otherwise, nobody understands how the risks crop up and sweep the project along issue after issue and suddenly a healthy project turns to red. Someone has rightly said, "Living at risk is jumping off the cliff and building your wings on the way down." A guideline document is required not only for the project team and the PM, but also for the customer and senior management to understand, manage, and control the project risks. Everyone involved in the project should follow the same process in order to have consistency in dealing with the risks and issues. Customers are often responsible for adding project risk, so they should be following the same process as the project team. This is important; otherwise, different groups will follow different directions, which will make it difficult to manage the risks. For this reason, the PM collects inputs from all stakeholders while preparing the project management plan, and particularly the risk management section. The PM should communicate the risk management plan to all key stakeholders and they should, in turn, approve of the risk management process. As a best practice, discuss the process and the procedure with the team members and other stakeholders to make them aware and understand the process clearly, and involve them in the preparation of the risk management plan.

The risk management plan, in general, contains the following information:

1. *Risk identification:* Documents and defines the process for identification of the risk. The project team, customers, users, and subject matter experts discuss and identify the risks that may impact the project objectives. This is an iterative process; the frequency of discussion may vary from project to project. The risk register of similar past projects should be reviewed to get a quick idea about potential risks. A risk register should be created and maintained as an output of this process. The risk register is updated for the individual risk against the risk category, potential response, and the root cause of the risk.

2. *Risk analysis:* Defines the approach for analyzing the identified risks in terms of categorization, impact, ranking, etc. This portion of the plan describes the tools and techniques to use for this process, along with the roles and responsibilities. The document should define the probability and impact and tailor them as per the needs and demands of the project. The probability–impact matrix is described in detail later in this book. Detail the scale of probability and impact, and create a probability–impact matrix for the project risk. The risk breakdown structure (RBS) is generally used for risk categorization. The RBS from a previous similar project can be used and tailored for a specific project need. Quantitative and qualitative analysis are common tools for performing the risk analysis task.

3. *Risk response planning:* Once the analysis is complete, the response plan should be prepared for each risk category or for each specific individual risk. This section details the strategy and action plan for different risk categories and describes what the action plan should be for the team before and after the risk occurs. Response could be acceptance, mitigation, avoidance, transfer, contingency planning, etc. Every response is elaborated in great detail in this section so that there is no ambiguity about the way the risks should be handled. Response planning depends on the tolerance level of the stakeholders with regard to the specific project and specific risk category. Risk tolerance may vary from project to project; this information should be obtained by talking to the customer and to senior management.

4. *Risk response implementation:* The project team should keep an eye on the symptoms and warnings of the risks and then execute the action plan as laid out in the previous section (risk response planning). Roles and responsibilities

are defined for every area so that the leads and supporting staff for every area monitor the events in their respective areas and take corrective action as per the procedure defined in the plan.

5. *Risk tracking:* Risks should be monitored and tracked regularly. Find out the status of the originally identified risks and change their status as required. Some new risks may need to be added from time to time as the project moves along and as the project team learns new things in the project. A risk register is generally created and maintained for this purpose. The project manager should take a lead in tracking the risk status on a weekly basis or at some other frequency. Tracking should not only happen for the identified risks but also for other aspects of the risk management, such as risk analysis, risk response planning, and execution.

6. *Risk reporting:* It is very important to report project risks and issues to the stakeholders on a regular basis. Format and frequency should be established in the risk management planning phase. Usually, risks are reported as part of the weekly status report and as part of the milestone report. The plan should include these details, along with the escalation process for every area and every risk category.

Strategies for Risk Response Planning

The strategy for managing a risk depends on whether it is an opportunity or a threat to any of the project objectives, such as scope, cost, time, quality, safety, security, etc. Apart from this, there are other considerations, such as the risk tolerance level of the customer and that of the senior management, cost–benefit, mission criticality, etc.

Strategy for Threat

As shown in Figure 2.6, there are mainly three kinds of strategies for threat situations:

1. *Avoid:* Under this strategy, the team plans to eliminate a particular risk altogether from the project. Avoidance may require extra cost, so the project manager should consider budget constraints of the project. This strategy can be implemented by changing the process or sometimes having the impacted project objective itself getting changed. For example, suppose an organization has only two in-house software engineers to work on a legacy technology. A strategic and critical software enhancement project requiring two software engineers can be implemented much faster using the legacy technology. But considering the high market demand for legacy engineers and the scarcity of such engineers in the organization, the company does not want to risk using legacy technology, fearing what will happen if they quit the company. So, to avoid the risk, the project decides to go with new technologies even though

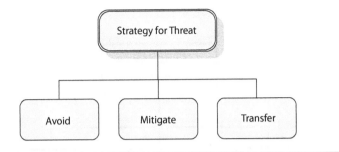

Figure 2.6 Strategy for threat.

it will require more work to build extra pieces to connect with the existing
system that is built on the legacy technology.

2. *Mitigate:* Risk has two components: probability and impact. Resultant is the
multiplication of probability and impact. In this strategy, either the risk probability or the impact is minimized, or sometimes both are reduced.

3. *Transfer:* Under this plan, the project organization shifts the liability of the
risk to a different party. This strategy does not eliminate or reduce the probability or the consequences of the risk, but rather transfers the responsibility of
managing the risk to some other organization. Insurance is the best example
of risk transfer where the project performing organization pays a premium to
the insurance company for bearing the result of the risk. In a fixed-bid project, the risk is transferred to the vendor. Insurance companies may re-insure
some of their high-risk programs/plans.

Strategy for Opportunity

There are three main risk response strategies for the positive risks (Figure 2.7):

1. *Exploit:* One would like to exploit the opportunity, but everything comes at
a price. Under this strategy, the project manager would attempt to remove all
uncertainties with the risk to make it happen.

2. *Enhance:* The impact and/or the probability of the risk is maximized, so the
size of the opportunity increases.

3. *Share:* If the company does not have the capability and resources to exploit
or enhance the opportunity, then it may tie up with another organization to
share the fruit of opportunity. For example, an automaker "A" ventures into
a new market to increase the market reach as well as to increase the revenue,
profit, and market share. However, it does not have the know-how about the
new market so it forms a partnership with an existing local automaker "B"
that takes care of the sales, marketing, and sales support of the products of
company "A" in the local market.

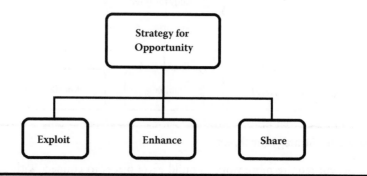

Figure 2.7   Strategy for opportunity.

Strategy for Threats and Opportunities

Accept: Sometimes a risk is known but the cost of realizing the opportunity or minimizing the threat outweighs the result of the risk, so the risk is accepted. It may also happen that the organization cannot do anything at all about the risk, so it accepts the risk. If nothing at all is done to the risk and it is accepted as it is, then that is called *passive acceptance*. On the other hand, if a contingency reserve is allocated to deal with the result once the risk occurs, then it is called *active acceptance*. The latter is called *contingent response strategy*, which involves the development of alternatives to deal with the situation once the risk occurs. A contingent reserve, also called a buffer, can be allotted in terms of cost, time, and resources to handle the after-effects.

Supporting Project Management Plans

Apart from the plans described above, a project management plan can have several other supporting plans, depending on the organization's process and project needs. Some of these plans could be the procurement management plan, configuration management plan, knowledge management plan, environmental management plan, security control plan, safety management plan, transition management plan, etc.

Procurement Management Plan

The organization may need to purchase or acquire products and/or services from an outside entity in order to carry out the work of the project. This is called procurement, which needs to be managed properly in order to manage the project successfully. Companies may not have the resources, expertise, and/or material available in-house to perform the entire work of the project. Sometimes, more than one vendor is engaged, so the project can have multiple contracts and sub-contracts that may need a lot of coordination effort. To administer project contracts and the purchase orders issued from the project, the project procurement management plan includes contract management and change management processes. The procurement management process involves contracts that are legal documents. A contract is a legal relationship subject to remedy in the courts. A contract describes the product and services features, the terms and conditions under which the work will be done, payment mode and frequency, and the process of performance evaluation apart from details of penalties and sanctions. A contract, being a legal document, needs review by and approval from legal experts, senior management, and experts from the procurement department. The project team should review the contract to ensure that the description of the product, service, timelines, and other technical details are good and as per the needs of the project.

The procurement management plan describes how the procurement processes will be managed and covers the entire life cycle of the contract—from the process of identification of contracting needs, to the vendor selection process, to contract administration, and finally to how the contract can be closed. The plan works as the guideline for the project manager, project team, and procurement department to carry out the procurement and contract work for the project.

The procurement management plan should include processes for the following:

1. *Identification of items needed for procurement:* WBS, resource planning, cost planning, and schedule planning provide input for the procurement needs. The company may lack the resources (labor or material supplies) to carry out certain work. Sometimes, labor and capital can be available at a cheaper rate that may provide a cost advantage to the project. At times, the organization may need to outsource the work to make it faster to meet the deadlines. The plan should describe the criteria for selecting procurement items, along with the justification.

2. *Contract types:* The procurement management plan mentions the types of contract that the project can have for different items. This should align with the organizational policy. Some common contract types include fixed-bid contract (also called fixed-price or lump-sum contract), cost-reimbursable contract, Time & Material (T&M) contract, etc. There can be many variations of these contract types.

3. *Vendor selection process:* There can be many criteria for evaluating the vendors, including past performance for similar work, brand name, technical capabilities, business size, relative cost, quality, proprietary rights, etc.

4. *Roles and responsibilities:* Identify roles and responsibilities for carrying out the various functions that procurement management may require on the project. This may include people from outside the project team, particularly for the review and approval process, vendor payments, etc.

5. *Assumptions and constraints:* List the assumptions and constraints that might affect the procurement process.

6. *Process of linking other project processes,* such as project scheduling, project cost management, resource management, quality management, performance management, to the procurement management process.

7. *Process for developing contract SOW and contract WBS:* Contract SOW includes portion of the project scope that is to be done outside of the organization. The project scope document and the WBS are the inputs for this document.

8. *Vendor performance evaluation process,* including the preparation of performance matrix, service level agreement, etc.

9. *Contract administration:* Document the process to make sure that both of the parties meet the obligation of the contract. Depending on the size of the contract and the process of the organization, contract administration is sometimes done by the administrative function separate from the project organization. Contract administration involves integration of the outputs from the contracted work into the overall work of the project and extending the project management process into the contracted work. For this purpose, contractors provide status and performance reports at predefined frequencies. The project team gets involved in the quality control of the contracted work, integrated change control, risk management for the contracted work, etc. Contract administration also deals with financial management of the contract.

10. *Contract closure:* Involves the administrative closure process for making sure that all the contracted work products are reviewed and approved; all invoices, payments, and claims are settled; lessons learned documents are prepared; audits are completed; and there are no open items remaining. This goes as input into the project closure process. Even if it is agreed that the contract will be terminated prematurely, administrative closure should be performed properly and the plan should describe a detailed process for carrying out this activity. Make sure that all the terms and conditions of the contract are duly met by both parties and that appropriate approval and signoffs are obtained.

Configuration Management (CM) Plan

Configuration management is a field of management study in itself and is very popular in software development projects. Compliance with CM practices is one of the requirements for getting CMMI level-2 certification for any IT organization. Sometimes people consider configuration management as a housekeeping system, such as the Five S concept used in manufacturing and inventory management. As a matter of fact, CM is much broader in scope and function than just housekeeping. The purpose of CM is to establish and maintain consistency in the performance of a product and to maintain its integrity. Major functions of configuration management consist of identification, control, auditing, and status accounting of the changes. The process ensures that changes to all the project deliverables and artifacts are controlled, audited, and authorized. The changes should be traceable by means of audit trails. CM is directly linked to the scope management and change management processes of the project.

The CM plan defines processes required to make sure that changes to the project deliverables occur within an identifiable and controlled environment. The document describes the configuration management tasks and activities to be exercised by the project team during the course of the project and typically includes the following:

1. *Scope:* Defines the scope of the configuration control; that is, it describes what deliverables and items will be controlled through configuration management. Configuration items may be customer deliverables, internal work products, and acquired products and tools. Configuration items can be identified based on criteria such as criticality of the work products, dependency of the work products on another, work products expected to change, work products that may be used by several groups, etc.

2. *Roles and responsibilities:* The plan defines roles and responsibilities and assigns names to the roles. The configuration management team essentially consists of a lead, a back-up, and other supporting staff. Identify the change control board members and its organization.

3. *CM process:* The plan describes in great detail the versioning processes, naming conventions, how the deliverables and artifacts are baselined for the first time, and then how they can be re-baselined after review and approval from required authorities. The CM plan explains the process for organizing the deliverables so that there is a place for everything and everything is in its place. The folder structure of the project share drive and the organization of the project sharepoint should be illustrated clearly. This process is very helpful because the artifacts are organized systematically and can be found quickly when they are needed. The document identifies kinds of users who require different levels of access (read, write, update, delete) for various artifacts and folders, and further explains the process for granting, revoking, and requesting access for different document, software, and servers. The plan provides information about the tools to be used for accomplishing CM tasks; for example, Visual Source Safe (VSS) is used for document control. The entire CM process section can be broken down into multiple subsections.

4. *Change control process:* It is linked to the change management plan.

5. *Review and audit process:* The plan should establish a process for CM audits in order to find gaps in the implementation of the plan and to suggest corrective action so that CM process works as desired. The process should explain the frequency of audit, items to be reviewed, roles of auditors and participants, and timelines for closing the open nonconformities found during the audit.

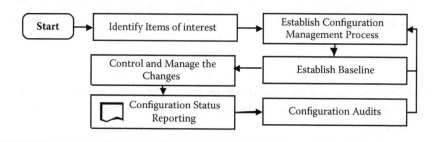

Figure 2.8 Flow of CM process.

Figure 2.8 illustrates the high-level process flow. As is evident, the configuration management plan in a project helps find answers to the following questions:

1. What artifacts need configuration control?
2. What is the process for making changes to the artifacts?
3. Who made the changes?
4. What changes were made?
5. When were the changes made?
6. Why were the changes made?
7. Who authorized the changes?

Projects use some kind of document control system to store project documents. In general, there is an organization-level usage guideline for the document control tool. This guideline can be tailored for project needs; otherwise it can be used as-is in the configuration management plan by referencing the guideline document. The document control usage guideline states the process of creating the project in the tool (such as VSS, Documentum, Clearcase, Qsmart, PVCS, Sharepoint, etc.). Projects generally have standard folder and subfolder names and structure. Check-in and check-out process, version numbering, and document retention versus archival processes are generally consistent with the organizational process. Either the CM lead from the project organization or some other document controller outside the project organization owns the document control system and related processes for the project. So, the project managers may not be involved in the day-to-day affairs of the CM process, but they should ensure the process is part of their plan. Execution, monitoring, and control should take place as per the defined process.

A CM audit is a very good tool for keeping the process under control. The audit should take place at least once for all team members. It should check the understanding of the team members regarding the check-in/check-out process, where they can find guidelines for reference purposes, what the version numbering process is, whether or not they are aware of the folder structure, whether or not their own deliverables are stored properly, and whether or not the naming standards have been followed. The auditor should also inquire where the team members are keeping their work-in-progress deliverables; the in-progress deliverables should also be checked-in every day at the end of the day so that there is a back-up of the artifact maintained and in the event of system failure or any other misadventure, the work can be restored from the back-up. Make sure the owner of the deliverable stores the signoff and approval emails/notes properly and in a timely fashion. A checklist for the audit should be prepared; this can be the part of the document control usage guideline or the CM plan. Audit results along with any nonconformity should be communicated by the auditor to the audited person, PM, and the corresponding team lead.

Consider a case of the requirements document for an information technology project. This is a critical work product that must be considered for the configuration control. When the owner of the document starts working on it, he/she names the draft version as per the version control process. The draft document is stored at the location specified in the CM plan. No one else has edit/write/delete access to the document except the owner. Others have read-only access. The revision history of the document is updated every time the document receives review comments from the reviewers. Finally, when the document is approved, it is baselined and the version number is changed to conform to the established versioning method (say, the version number is V1.0). Nobody is allowed to make any changes to the document thereafter. If the need for a change arises, the PM submits a change control. Upon approval of the change control, the requirements document is checked out and the changes are made. The version number changes at this time to show an intermediate version number as per the versioning method described in the CM plan (that is, V1.01). The updated document again goes through the review process. When the document is approved for the new changes, the requirements document is re-baselined with a new version number (that is, V1.1). No one is allowed to make changes, however small they may be, to this version unless another change control is submitted and approved. Same configurable items should not be stored at multiple places because this will create integrity issues, confusion, and extra work.

Knowledge Management (KM) Plan

Knowledge is power. This fact also holds true for corporations and organizations. Organizations have realized that knowledge management is necessary for the purpose of performance improvement, competitive advantage, agility, and innovation. Knowledge management includes practices and business activities related to the identification, creation, storage, distribution, and measurement of knowledge assets. Exchange of knowledge is the focus in the entire exercise. In the current, fast-paced business world, things are changing very rapidly, products and processes are getting more and more complex, and teams are very dynamic in nature. All these factors necessitate the need for a formal knowledge management strategy for the organization. Business must keep pace with the changes happening around it. In the face of a global business environment, it is essential to keep the dependency on personal knowledge as low as possible. Employees and organizational units are encouraged to document their knowledge and experience so that others benefit, and the knowledge is not lost once the employees leave the organization. Others can build on to the documented knowledge.

Knowledge management is not just restricted to the documentation of personal or an organization's knowledge. It covers a broader area of knowledge, including research and development, the creation of tools and other creative methods to improve production and productivity, the spread of knowledge through mentoring and training, etc. Organizations cannot afford to reinvent the wheel every time. KM is an important part of all industries these days, and it is absolutely essential for knowledge-based industries, such as consulting, software, etc. KM is part and parcel of the normal work of employees in many organizations. Participation in KM activities such as the creation, review, update, and usage of KM artifacts is mandatory in many organizations because this is one of the tasks in an employee's appraisal evaluation, compensation determination, and scorecard. Goals are set for the organization that percolate down to unit-level goals, down to individual KM goals. Organization should have a mission, vision, policy, and procedure for knowledge management. There should be a detailed process for the creation, review, usage, and storage of the artifacts. For example, the organization can have a website for the storage of knowledge artifacts. There can be a KM committee that oversees the administrative activities of the process. Any new knowledge artifact needs to be submitted to the committee by filling out the proposal document. Once the proposal is evaluated and considered for review, the artifact can be submitted for review along with suggestions for the name of reviewers. The KM committee manages the logistics and processes of review, approval, and storage. Upon final review, the artifact can be posted on the website. Anyone can search for tools, documents, and artifacts on the website, just as one does a normal Web search on Google, Yahoo!, etc. Every click to the KM website can be recorded automatically and contributors can be awarded points for every use of the artifact. Some organizations maintain a KM tracker, which essentially has the names of team members, a list of their activities during a particular cycle (month, quarter, etc.), and a corresponding KM score. Evaluation criteria and scoring rules are predefined. At the end of the cycle, the KM champion can be announced and awarded.

The project knowledge management plan describes how the project will adhere to the KM policies, goals, and practices of the organization. A lessons learned exercise is linked to KM. To this effect, the plan includes the following:

1. *Scope:* What kind of KM artifacts are expected to be produced by the different functions inside the project: This should go as a task into the WBS and finally into the schedule of the project so that the timeline is determined and communicated to the team. Once the task is tracked at the WBS and schedule level, then it will also come under the scanner during the effort/cost esti-

mate of the project. It is essential to consider KM activities during the effort estimation exercise; otherwise there will be a gap in the cost and budget.

2. *Roles and responsibilities:* The KM plan defines the lead, back-up, and supporting roles for KM activities in the project. The KM team will guide the artifact creation, review, and storing process. PMO administrative staff or the organization's KM staff can assist in these roles and responsibilities.

3. *KM Process:* This section describes where the drafts should be created, the method of communication, how the review will take place, and, finally, where and how the artifacts will be stored so that they become part of the organization's knowledge asset. Tools and technologies involved in the KM process for generation and tracking of the artifact are explained. The process also defines reward and recognition methods. The project plan can reference the KM process document of the organization for the purpose of this section. If there are deviations, then a tailoring document can be prepared.

Transition Plan

This is a plan that helps in managing transitions in the project. Projects do not run forever; there must be a transition at the end of the project. The transition could be required with the business units, customer, a different vendor, operations and maintenance unit of the organization, etc. This is one of those activities that PMs usually neglect. However, if the transition is not done properly, it may lead to tremendous trouble for the end users and customers. This may have an impact on the business of the organization and result in internal conflict and friction. Typically, the transition plan describes how project deliverables will be brought to full operational status, integrated into ongoing operations, and maintained. The plan provides details about the following:

1. *Business processes and deliverables that need to be transitioned:* The plan should describe the current business process and what the end state would be. The document identifies all the deliverables (products and services) that will be transitioned to the other party, who approves these deliverables before the transition takes place.

2. *Roles and responsibilities of all the parties involved in transition:* List the roles and responsibilities for not only those imparting the transition, but also for those receiving the transition.

3. *Process for outlining transition task and schedule:* The details of the task and schedule may not be available at the beginning of the project. So, at that time, major tasks and schedule information should be included, and a process should be defined for detailing the information. Later, all the tasks are outlined and a full-fledged schedule is developed as per the guidelines documented and referenced in the transition plan.

4. *Transition budget:* It is very important that the transition activities and time-lines are considered while developing project estimates.
5. *Tools and technologies required for transition.*
6. *Communication process with regard to the project transition:* This section of the plan outlines how often and in what format the project progress, issues, and concerns will be communicated to various parties receiving the transition. In general, they are not required to be informed about every detail of the project, and the frequency of progress update is comparatively less. Identify the needs for transition meetings and their participants. The group receiving the transition may attend one meeting during the project kickoff. Later, they may be called to attend phase gate or exit gate meetings. The activity intensifies toward the end of the project where all the parties are invited to attend implementation meetings. The customer, business unit, and the operations team sign off on the transition plan document, implementation plan document, as well as the final product and services.
7. *Contractual obligations,* if any.

PMs usually start the transition activity toward the end of the project, which is not a good practice. The process should start at the beginning of the project. A high-level transition period should be identified in the beginning of the project. This should be documented in the project kickoff meeting agenda. Key stakeholders who will receive the transition should be invited into the project kickoff. This is a notification to all concerned that the organization has started such an initiative and they should be prepared to support the initiative once the project is finished. This will help the other party plan for the budget and resources (human resource, material supplies, etc.). Quite often, the project team will receive a lot of valuable information from these groups that helps in better design and planning.

Operations or external vendors will not take care of the project deliverables from day one when the deliverable is ready. Typically, the project team supports the business products and services for one week, one month, one quarter, or one year after the project is commissioned, and is based on the type of product, business situation, and contract. The time period depends on the type of industry, the nature of the project, and other variables. The project is not considered complete until the transition activity is finished. This generally overlaps with the project closing phase. In software development projects, this phase is usually called the post implementation phase. Note that projects are not always transitioned after product deployment. The performing organization may decide to quit midway through the project as per the clause of the contract, or the customer may ask the vendor to stop working on the contract and transition the work to a different vendor. These situations generally arise due to quality, financial, and proprietary concerns.

In software development projects, the implementation plan document usually works as the transition plan and describes the steps necessary to turn the project's product or service over to the business unit, customer, operations, and maintenance.

Environmental Management Plan (EMP)

Business cannot be separated from the natural environment. Increased awareness of the need to protect the environment has led to stringent environmental regulations for businesses, new and old. More and more companies across the globe are proactively trying to adopt environmental management systems, and they are striving for ISO 14001 and other environmental management certifications. If the project potentially affects the environment, then it must have an environmental management plan. IT projects do not typically need this plan but manufacturing, construction, and mining projects, for example, generally need to have EMPs as part of their project plans. The EMP describes the processes that the project will follow to maximize its compliance with local environmental policies and minimize harm to the environment. The level of detail will vary, depending on the need of the project and the maturity of the organization with respect to compliance with environmental responsibilities and regulations. Sometimes, the EMP must be submitted to the state environment department. The project can start only after review by and approval from the concerned state department. So, in such cases, the EMP becomes one of the most important and one of the main deliverables in a successful project.

The plan should clearly explain the steps required to adhere to the organization's and state's environmental policies. It explores how project activities and the products generated by the project could possibly affect the environment, both positively and negatively, and illustrates procedures to implement those environmental policies, including review and inspection of environmental factors and corrective actions required. The EMP identifies roles, responsibilities, resources, timelines, budget, training needs, and management commitment required to implement the plan. The plan should identify the quality goals for environmental factors such as air quality, water quality, noise level, forestation, etc. It should explain the process of taking corrective action so that the project activities and the result of the project do not deteriorate the quality beyond the accepted level. For example, a surface mining (also called open cast mining) project can deteriorate the air quality and water quality of the surroundings. It may affect the forestation, flora, and fauna and can create excessive noise in the surroundings. For such mining projects, the plan should identify the accepted level of dust density in the air for the work area and for the surrounding locality, and should identify corrective actions (such as using water sprinklers, dust suppressants, distribution of nose masks to workers, etc.) to control the air quality and exposure. Plantations around the mining area can further prevent the dust from flying out to residential areas and will also prevent excessive noise levels. The plan should mention the types of heavy, earth moving machines to be used in the project, the noise level (in decibels) generated by such machines, and how the operators and other workers can be protected by the use of earmuffs, headgear, and frequent breaks during work. The mining project requires a lot of water; the plan should explain the amount of water required for the project, where it is supplied from, the effect of this usage on the surrounding water table, and how the project will ensure minimum impact to the water table. The plan should explain how much water will be recirculated into the system, where the industrial waste will be dumped, waste treatment arrangements in order to minimize the impact, etc. Once the project is completed, the company cannot abandon the site as a wasteland. As part of the environmental management plan, it should identify the layout, timelines, resources, and budget for the reclamation of the land and the forest it used for the project. If treated properly, the value of the land can increase after the reclamation. There are many cases where some finished opencast mines were converted to a lake surrounded by nice, beautiful parks to make it a recreation facility for the locals as well as visitors.

One of the important aspects of the environmental management plan is the *disaster recovery plan* (DRP). Irrespective of the nature of the industry, if a project is required to have an EMP, then the EMP must contain a DRP. The DRP is the subset of the business continuity plan. Again, consider the surface mining project as the example. The DRP should explain the potential disasters caused by project work. The wastewater disposal line might burst, causing serious water contamination in the surroundings; a fire might break out in a machine or other mining facility that may be dangerous for the workers and surrounding environment; landslides can cause major problems (loss of life and property, blockage of the natural course of water, damage to the forest and plantation cover, loss of working hours, etc). The DRP, part of the EMP, should identify potential disaster situations and should explain the readiness plans of the project in terms of procedure, training plans, human resource, equipment, budget, etc.

Change Request Document

Change management is part of the integration management knowledge area. Organizations usually have a template for this communication tool. The PM prepares the change request (also called *change control*) document, often with the help of team members. Once the project team recognizes a change to the baseline version of *scope, schedule, and cost*, the PM documents the details and requests the change control board to review and approve the document. The project change control board would generally consist of the business owner, project sponsor, and steering committee members. Until the change request is approved, it is not considered part of the project plan, and the project team should continue working according to the original plan. Suppose the request is for additional project scope; then the team should not start working on the new scope until the change request is formally approved. Similarly, if the project team recognizes the need for additional cost in order to finish work for the existing scope, then no work should be carried out beyond the previously approved budget until the new budget is signed off. Ensure that the document has enough detail so that it helps the review board to make an informed, appropriate, and quick decision. Once the change request is signed off, it becomes part of the plan. The PM should reflect this change in the project plan by changing the version number of the original plan.

The change request document typically covers the following information:

1. *Project name and project number.*
2. *Author:* Generally the project or program manager.
3. *Date when the change request was raised.*
4. *Names of review board or change control board members.*
5. *Information about the project:* Project objectives, current schedule, and budget.
6. *Does the change apply to scope, schedule, cost, or more than one of these?*
7. *What is the change?* Provide a summary of the change compared to the baseline of the project scope, schedule, and cost, as the case may be. The information should be documented in a few sentences only; at the same time, it should not leave out any important point.
8. *Need/justification for the change:* Explain why the change is required and what value would the change add to the current functionality and to the originally identified business objectives.
9. *Financial and business impact of not doing the change:* Explain the impact on the project's business objectives if the change in not applied.
10. *Information on other alternatives explored:* Senior management will always be looking for the creativity of the project team and would like to understand the alternatives to the solutions. So brainstorm with the project team and the business users to identify alternatives and weigh the pros and cons of every alternative. Subject matter experts can be interviewed to obtain this detail. In case no alternatives are available, document that too.
11. *The financial, schedule, and business impacts of pursuing the change:* This is a very important piece of information for executives before making a go/no-go decision. Get estimations from the team for all the tasks to make the required change. Quite often, the information may be required immediately and the team may need to perform an analysis before giving a good estimate, but the project team may not have the bandwidth to carry out the required analysis. In such a case, ask for a ballpark estimate and communicate this fact clearly in the change request document. Mention the milestone schedules that may be impacted because of the change and provide the original and revised start and finish dates for those milestones. Similarly, prepare a comparison matrix for the relevant original business scope versus the revised business scope.
12. *Risks and assumptions associated with the change:* Risk can be positive as well as negative. Positive risk is the opportunity that the organization gets by making the change. Mention the negative risks for the change in terms of dependencies, cost, schedule, etc. Describe the risks in meeting the proposed change;

mention the probability of the risk and its impact. If you are proposing a change to the schedule, then describe all the risks in meeting the new schedule. This document should also list the new risks that this change would bring to the project objectives. Apart from this, revisit the existing risks of the project to assess if the change control will affect any of the existing risks. Assumptions made to meet the new schedule should be clearly pointed out in this document. This helps senior management in making a decision about the change request.

13. *Names of approvers, their organization, contact information, and the date they approved the document.*
14. *Project deliverables that require an update because of the change:* Invariably, the scope document, design document, project management plan, etc. should go through changes. Once the changes are made, approvals are required for the new version.

Project Status Report

This is one of the most important documents that a PM creates almost every week. In general, every organization has a template for the report and there is not much room to tinker with the format. Despite this, the PM must ensure that the format and frequency of the report is discussed and agreed upon by the customers in the communication planning phase of the project.

The status report typically includes information regarding the following:

1. Name of the report.
2. *As-of date:* Make sure the report produces status as of the reporting date itself. In general, there is a fixed date on which the PM must provide the status. For example, the PM may be required to provide a status report every Monday for the project status as of the previous Friday. Sometimes, for some reason or another, the report distribution may be delayed until, say, Wednesday or Thursday instead of Monday. In that case, it is also quite appropriate to report the status as of the previous Friday only until specifically asked by the stakeholders to report it for the current date. The reason for this is that it is always good to keep the report frequency the same so that the progress can be compared reasonably well.
3. *Who is reporting, or the name of the project manager.*
4. *Major stakeholders:* It is a good idea to mention the major stakeholders in the project. Mention the names and organization of the project sponsor, business owner, program manager, program director, steering committee members, etc.
5. *Overall status color (generally GREEN, YELLOW, RED, or BLUE):* Provide a proper comment on the status if it is YELLOW or RED, and provide the get to GREEN plan. Most of the time, organizations have explicit criteria for

what is considered BLUE, GREEN, YELLOW, or RED. If there is none, get them clarified from the PMO or the project governing body and distribute the information to all stakeholders as part of communication plan.

6. *Executive summary or executive attention:* Write special messages that executives should pay attention to. This should be a quick, short summary about the project status and the information that executives should know. Some of the best practices on this section are described later in more detail.

7. *Tasks planned for the reporting period:* State whether or not the tasks planned in the reporting week/month were achieved. If they were not achieved, add a comment stating the reason why they did not finish. This is also called the achievements made during the reporting period.

8. *Goal for the next reporting period:* Specify the tasks planned for next reporting period.

9. *Risks or issues, including management/executive attention:* If the list is too long, cite the major current risks and then provide a link or location to the entire list.

10. *Major milestones, their planned/actual start and end dates, status and percent completion, and comments or remarks:* If a particular task is in YELLOW or RED status, provide a short, appropriate comment on why it is not GREEN, how it affects the overall status, what it will take to make it GREEN, and what is being done to that effect. Present the milestone information in tabular form for better visual presentation.

11. *It is always good to provide status on cost and budget.*

The project will generally involve multiple application areas within the organization, or sometimes it will involve multiple units within the same application area. Every application area or unit can have different challenges (in terms of resource, budget, scope, risk, etc.) and dependencies; and in the case that they are managed as one project, it is imperative as well as easy to report the status of these individual application/subject areas separately, although in the same report document. Make different sections for their milestones. The overall status of the project will depend on the status of all these application/subject areas. For example, if the project has three application (Apps) areas without any dependencies with each other: Apps 1 is planned to finish in six months, Apps 2 in eight months, and Apps 3 in twelve months. The business owner and sponsor do not mind as long as all three projects finish by the end of twelve months. Now suppose that we are in the ninth month and Apps 1 and 3 are in GREEN status but Apps 2 is in RED status because of the lack of sufficient resources to start the implementation activity. It is expected that the required resources will be available after one month and to finish the task by the end of the tenth month. So, in this case, even though the status of Apps 2 will be reported as RED (because the implementation date has been missed), the overall status can still be reported as GREEN because the project is expected to accomplish its schedule objective of implementing all three application areas in twelve months.

Be extra careful while writing special messages intended for senior management. Keep the message short and simple, appear positive, and indicate options you have tried to overcome challenges. Avoid open-ended statements and provide ETA (expected turnaround) for every pending decision or action that you cite in this section. For example, suppose someone writes "Completion of design is pending inputs from lead architect." It is quite evident that this information is incomplete because it does not tell when the input from architect will be available. This makes the executives curious. You can expect questions from senior management on such reports. To avoid such unnecessary questions, keep your report full and complete by providing the necessary ETA. In case the ETA is not available, then also report that. So, a better report would state: "Completion of design is pending inputs from lead architect, which is expected to be available by 12/1. Attempt is being made to engage another senior architect for faster turnaround." The message should neither be offensive toward any organization, group, or stakeholder, nor be defensive about you. It is very common to get carried away in the blame game when a project faces a crisis, but one should always stay away from such a trap.

Following are some more tips to make a better project status report:

1. The report should not be too long, but at the same time, it should contain enough details to provide sufficient information for decision making. Long reports will discourage readers to go through every detail and so they might miss some vital information.

2. Keep the format of the report simple so that it is easy to read and maintain. Avoid too many colors, too many fonts, too many styles, and too much animation.

3. Do not hide any vital information—due to fear or any other reason. Executives will find it sooner or later, and it may backfire. More importantly, if executives get the information (good or bad) on time, they will help you or will suggest ways to overcome the challenges. That does not mean you should include every tiny detail. Keep the statements neutral and positive.

4. Work with the stakeholders and customers to provide them with the information they need.

5. Spend enough time in preparation and self-review of the report because this is one of the most important deliverables that has far-reaching impact on performance evaluation.

6. Do print previews before distribution and ensure contents appear properly so that they are easily readable. If you are using colors, they may appear very nice on a computer screen but when printed, they might not appear that good. Not everyone has a color printer; for the benefit of such readers, supplement the color with the name of the color or its abbreviation.

7. If the report uses a macro or formula to compute the values of some fields for generating a result (especially if using MS Excel), then check the formula and the macro every time you make a change to any of the fields that are used in the macro.

You may have put so much time and energy into writing the report every week, yet no one has ever come back to you with a question or concern. Some PMs may feel happy about it, but in fact it is not a healthy sign. The status report is a very powerful tool for the project manager, so the PM must ensure that the effort does not go down the drain. One of the ways to overcome this challenge is to set up a regular meeting with the stakeholders to go through the report. If that is not possible, at least copy the main contents (executive summary section, major risks and issues section, etc.) of the report into the body of an email such that the email does not exceed more than one page. This will provide others with a taste of your report for quick review without requiring them to open the document. If they are interested in getting more details, they will be lured into opening the report and reading it thoroughly. There are chances that you may be asked to modify the report format or content. Show openness for such changes after understanding why they want the change. After all, you are writing the report to provide the information stakeholders need and the information that you want them to know. Different people like different formats, so in the case of conflict, go with the choice of the main stakeholder; others need to work with him or her.

Milestone Report

Projects are typically reviewed by executives at the end of major milestones. These are the checkpoints where projects are monitored to keep them on track. In real life, a milestone is a marker that tells how far you are from a certain point—so you know how far you have traveled toward your destination and how much farther you have to travel. Project milestones perform exactly this role in a project schedule. They mark significant events, deliverables, or interdependencies that need to be monitored to keep the project on track. A project milestone report provides information about what has been achieved and what else should be done to successfully complete the project. Milestone reporting is just one of many ways to monitor and present the status of a project. It is an extremely effective approach in large and complex projects with many interdependencies because it helps present information in a meaningful yet concise way, showing what has actually been achieved.

The first step is to identify the major and critical milestones so that they can be used for better tracking and control of the project. The milestone report typically provides information about the current milestones, their status (whether or not they are on track), slippages if any, reasons for slippage, and the risks associated with the current and future milestone tasks. Project scheduling tools, such as MS Project, have features available to earmark certain tasks as milestone tasks. A milestone task does not have any effort associated with it. These tasks can be imported through the tool into a different document, which can readily provide information about all milestone tasks for the project, date of completion, and their percent completion. Take baseline (original) and revised dates for the milestones from the project schedule. A simple milestone report only contains the name of major deliverables, their status, along with comments. However, a perfect milestone report should go beyond that and should also report risk and issue status, defect summary, budget status, resource status, etc., at every milestone. A project risk register can be attached to the milestone report. Figure 2.9 provides an example of a sample milestone report prepared in MS Excel. Note that milestones in *italics* represent customer responsibilities and those in normal font are the responsibilities of the performing organization. This can very well belong in Chapter 4 (tables and metrics). However, the format of the report can vary from organization to organization, or project to project, and sometimes it might very well be presented in text format using MS Word or other such tool.

Meeting Agenda and Meeting Minutes Document

Project managers spend most of their time in meetings. They need to interact with cross-functional teams in these meetings and it is PM's job to keep the participants focused on the meeting objective, prevent conflicts, extract the right kind of information, and, finally, come out from the meeting with the achieved objectives. If not managed properly, the meetings will be chaotic and will create hindrances for the project. The meeting agenda and meeting minutes are two very powerful communication tools at a PM's disposal. It is good practice to send an agenda to the participants before the meeting and follow up the meeting with minutes. However, that is not enough; a good agenda and good minutes are as essential for the success of the meeting as any other factor. There is a famous proverb: *"A good lather is half the shave."* Plan the meeting in advance as much as possible and put in the effort in preparing for important meetings.

Many people may argue that meeting minutes are overkill; however, on big and complex projects, many decisions are made in the meetings and if not documented and stored properly, some important decisions might fall through the cracks. One can refer to them in the future for tracking the history of important and critical issues. Above all, it serves the purpose of fair understanding among the participants to ensure that everyone is on the same page as far as understanding and agreement are concerned. In case the understanding of the PM is not correct, then it can be corrected by other participants through a revision of the minutes. Sometimes, all the participants may not be able to attend the meeting. In such cases, the minutes of a meeting make everyone aware of the discussion, decisions made, and next steps.

The agenda should generally contain the following:

Milestones	Original End Date	Revised End Date	Actual End Date	Status	Original Budget	Revised Budget	Actual Cost	Risk (H, M, L)	Comments
Initiation	31-Oct-08	14-Nov-08	11-Nov-08	Complete	$8,000	$10,000	$10,500		
Receive specimen from customer	14-Nov-08	14-Nov-08	21-Nov-08	Complete	$0	$0	$0		
Staff core project team	14-Nov-08	14-Nov-08	10-Nov-08	Complete	$0	$0	$0		
Staff consulting team (Customer)	14-Nov-08	14-Nov-08	10-Nov-08	Complete	$0	$0	$0		
Business requirement	31-Dec-08	31-Dec-08	25-Jan-09	Complete	$75,000	$95,000	$100,000		Specimen was changed after several rounds of initial discussion.
Design	20-Feb-09	27-Feb-09		In Progress	$200,000	$265,000		H	Status Red - Lead designer left organization while one of the supporting designers got sick.
Finalize vendor requirements	12-Jan-09	12-Jan-09	12-Jan-09	Complete	$5,000	$5,000	$4,000	L	*—continued*

Figure 2.9 An example of a sample milestone report prepared in MS Excel.

			In Progress				Status Green - On Track
Secure vendor resources	6-Feb-09	6-Feb-09		$10,000	$10,000	L	Use extra resources to catch up schedule. High Risk because budget impacted negatively. Medium Risk for Schedule.
Construction	22-May-09	22-May-09		$450,000	$600,000	H	
Quality testing	30-Jun-09	30-Jun-09		$150,000	$150,000		Overlap this task with Construction to reduce impact on final schedule.
User acceptance testing	17-Jul-09	17-Jul-09		$40,000	$40,000		Overlap this task with Quality testing to reduce impact on final schedule.
Commission the product	7-Aug-09	7-Aug-09		$20,000	$20,000		
Project closure	21-Aug-09	21-Aug-09		$10,000	$10,000		

Figure 2.9 (continued) An example of a sample milestone report prepared in MS Excel.

1. *Subject of the meeting.*
2. *Date and time:* Include time zone information because participants might be located in different time zones across the globe.
3. *Location:* Use Web access information if the meeting is webcasted and use dial-in information if it is a conference call. These two are invariably always used these days because of the international nature of the business as participants are located remotely.
4. *Organizer:* This is the host of the meeting.
5. *Participants:* Add information about the organization or designation and project role of each participant if required. This is particularly helpful when the participants are new to each other.

The table in Figure 2.10 nicely captures the points discussed above and it does not take much space. While sending the agenda before the meeting, the name of attendees can just be mentioned in the normal font as shown in the figure. After the meeting, when you distribute minutes, just mark the attendees by making their names bold or by highlighting with some color as per convenience.

6. *Discussion points in order of priority:* Sometimes you need to make them flexible as per the availability of key participants. For example, if a key participant is available only for the first 10 minutes of the meeting, then it makes sense to discuss those items first for which you need input from that participant.
7. *Agenda items should be presented in concise bullet format as much as possible:* Benefits include better presentation, making sure that nothing is missed, and provides an opportunity for allocating time against each agenda item.
8. *Open action items from the last meeting (if applicable) in case of a follow-up meeting or a recurring meeting:* This will ensure follow-ups take place regularly and the action items do not fall through.

Host	Shankar Jha	Location	Conf-room A-100
Date/Time	11/18/2008 9:30–10:30 (GMT)	**Call-in info**	1-800-888-9999 Access Code 1234
Attendees – Participants who attended the meeting are in bold.	Attendee A; Attendee B; Attendee C; Attendee D; Attendee E		

Figure 2.10 Meeting agenda document.

9. *If the purpose of the meeting is to discuss some issue or problem and to choose the best option to resolve it, then clearly outline "Background/Event," "Problem Statement," "Impact," and "Options or Possible Resolutions"*: If this information can be available before the meeting, it saves a lot of time and keeps the meeting on track. This is just an example that can be extended to any other discussion topic. Bottom line: good, structured documentation enhances the chances of success, saves enormous amounts of time (remember: a meeting is normally attended by multiple people so even a fifteen-minute savings in meeting time saves a lot of man-hours collectively), and helps keep the participants' morale high.

For a regular team meeting (e.g., weekly project team meeting), it is a good idea to keep administrative items at the top of the agenda as a regular item to discuss with the team. Examples of the administrative items include when the timesheet is due every week, location or path of project documents, vacation time (PTO time) of project team members, special organizational announcements made recently that may concern the project or the project team, any other administrative items that team members need to be aware of or need to be reminded, etc.

The minutes of meeting document should contain the following:

1. *Participants who attended the meeting:* To avoid double writing, you can highlight with some color the names of participants mentioned in the agenda document.
2. *Discussion and decision points in a concise format against every agenda item:* Again, there is no need to write this separately; mention the discussion points just below the agenda item; you may just keep the font color different to distinguish between the agenda and the minutes. This will keep the document concise, reduce your time in preparing the minutes, and save time for readers because they do not have to go through multiple pages and read the same thing over and over again. You may notice that people invariably do not read the meeting minutes document, one reason being that they become discouraged when they see a multipage document. Figure 2.11 provides an example of how a meeting agenda and minutes can be documented in one place only without duplication.
3. *Action item, owner, due date, and status (open/close):* Use a table to better organize the action item. Care should be taken to have one owner for an action item (Figure 2.12). If more than one person is responsible for the task, then one owner should be identified who will take the lead in completing the task with the support of others.

Use a Word document for meeting minutes and attach it in an email rather than documenting the minutes in the email itself—unless the content is short enough to accommodate in less than a page of email. Some organizations use an

Agenda in Italic font and minutes in normal font.

Agenda 1

    Minutes 1

    1. Agenda 2

    Minutes 2

    2. Agenda 3

    Minutes 3

    3. Agenda 4

    Minutes 4

Figure 2.11 An example of how a meeting agenda and minutes can be documented in one place only without duplication.

Item #	Action Item	Owner	Due Date	Status (Open/Close)

Figure 2.12 Action items.

MS Excel template for meeting agendas and minutes, but one will find that MS Word is better suited for this purpose.

It is not essential that the PM takes notes in the meeting or that he/she sends the minutes; this task can be delegated to an appropriate person. Sometimes the discussions can be too technical for a PM to understand everything clearly or to take appropriate notes. So, in these cases, the task can be delegated; however, as much as possible, the PM should take notes and should prepare the minutes himself, particularly when it is a cross-functional meeting or a status meeting. The reason is very simple: there are so many things discussed in the meeting that everything might not be relevant for documentation. Participants who are experts in different functions will think in their own way and may align the minutes as they perceive the issue. The PM is a neutral person who has a broad view, so a PM can avoid extra details, and at the same time all the necessary elements can be captured and distributed. Many PMs use administrative assistants for taking notes and for distributing meeting minutes. Administrators do not have the insight so they may either capture everything, including all the noise from the meeting, or may leave out critical points due to a lack of understanding. The use of administrative assistants should be avoided in this case. As a best practice, apart from timely distribution, meeting minutes should also be stored at a fixed location as per the configuration management plan or the document control system of the project. Use admin for the purposes of document maintenance and storage.

Project Closure Report

Projects must be closed formally and properly. Formal closure is as important as formal initiation. This is one process that often gets a raw deal. The team is in a hurry to get out of all project activities and is looking forward to the next assignment. However, the PM should ensure that the intensity is maintained and people take part in activities with enthusiasm. The closing process might involve many tasks, based on the process of the organization. A few, common examples include signing off on emails from customers, wrapping up administrative documentation, final audit signoff, final lessons learned documentation and discussion, contract close-out, transition and handover to maintenance and operations, etc. Sometimes the project closure report refers to a checklist and sometimes it documents in itself the list of tasks required to be completed in order to formally finish the project closure process. One will be able to close the project in a professional and efficient manner by completing the steps listed in the document.

It is very important for a project manager to prepare and send a closure report to all stakeholders and upper management. This gives the PM a chance to showcase the achievements of the project. Although a project has faced many issues and struggles, they may be presented as challenges and one can mention what the project team did to overcome those challenges. People generally remember failures, so it is also important to make everyone aware of the successes. Therefore, it is an opportunity to change the perception of people positively in your favor about the project and its success despite numerous challenges. There is a famous saying: "All's well that ends well."

The project closure report generally includes the following:

1. *Objectives of the project*, including which objectives were met and which ones were not met. Provide appropriate remarks for the objectives not fully met by the project. Mention how these objectives will be taken care of. Sometimes, it may become part of some other project or may be taken into the scope of the next phase of the same project.
2. *Signoffs* from customers, operations, production and maintenance department, and all other required authorities.
3. *List of deliverables* produced and their location in the project library.

4. *List of open items and who is taking care of those* after closure of the project.
5. *Success stories:* This is different from the objectives mentioned in (1.) above. This section should explain what the project team did to overcome challenges and to sail through the crisis situation. Highlight the achievements of the project and those of the project team without going overboard.
6. *Lessons learned:* Good practices, areas of improvements, and recommendations. This is explained in great detail as a separate topic in this chapter.
7. *Report on schedule and cost:* Provide proper comment on variances.
8. *List of change requests.*
9. *Contracts and invoices,* if applicable.
10. *Contributors:* Mention the names of project team members from various functional organizations. Also mention the names of other stakeholders and their organizations.

Most importantly, do not forget to appreciate the team. Special appreciation can go to some selected members, who went above and beyond to contribute exceptionally to make a positive difference in the project, but a general appreciation should go to everyone. It is recommended that the special appreciation should be sent separately, explaining why their contributions are appreciated.

Projects may end prematurely; it is more important to close such projects properly to avoid confusion at a later stage about what was achieved by the project and what was not achieved. In such a situation, document the reason behind early close-out, project phases that were completed along with the last project phase, objectives met, objectives remaining to be met, authorization note from the sponsor to close out the project, list of deliverables produced along with all the signoffs, deliverables produced partly, deliverables not produced at all, cost and budget details, contract closure signoffs, lessons learned document, success stories, list of change requests, contributors, etc.

Many organizations have a *toll gate, exit gate,* or *phase gate* process at certain milestones. In general, the members of upper management are the key participants in a toll gate review. Depending on the process of the organization projects qualifying, some predetermined criteria must be presented at the toll gate at certain milestones or events. Examples of the criteria for qualifying for a toll gate include: projects exceeding $1.0 million in budget must go through the toll gate at the end of planning phase; any project exceeding the OOM estimate at the end of the design phase by more than 50 percent; or all regulatory projects must go through the toll gate at the end of the planning, design, and testing phase, etc. Similarly, if an organization follows an exit gate process, then projects must go through the phase gate or exit gate for a review of different critical parameters at the end of every phase. The concept described in the project closure report is also applicable to a toll gate report or exit gate report. The content might change a little bit but the concept remains the same. It is good practice to prepare and distribute such a report at the end of every major milestone.

There are many benefits of exit gate reports. One of the most important benefits is the recognition by team members and stakeholders of the closure of the previous phase. This gives the PM a chance to obtain acceptance and approval signoffs from the customer and other stakeholders on the deliverables produced in the previous phase, obtain required deliverables from the other applications and organizations that may be required in the next phase, and also obtain approval from the customer and the stakeholders to proceed with the next phase. The logical break given by the exit gate provides the project team with an opportunity to review their successes and failures in the previous phase, discuss lessons learned, re-estimate the work of the next phases, and, if required, reset goals and re-baseline the project plan. Project performance should be reviewed thoroughly at the end of a phase. This is also a good time for different kinds of project audits. Sometimes the phases may overlap or there may not be a hard break between two phases. In that case, the phase gate review should be conducted as soon as the important deliverables of the previous phase are ready. Also record the ongoing work of the next phase in the phase gate review report.

Lessons Learned Document

A project, by its nature, is full of lessons for the team members and the organization. Things seldom go as per the plan, but that does not mean one should stop planning or stop learning. Planning and execution get better in an organization with experience. So, it is imperative that the project team keeps learning from every lesson and also captures the lessons and passes them on to the process assets of the organization so that others are benefited on future projects. Not many organizations are mature enough to realize this benefit, which results in their poor learnability as an organization and the projects keep making the same mistakes time and again.

This is another neglected process in the project, the reason being that this document does not have a direct impact on the deliverables of the ongoing project in most cases. If at all, people prepare a document for the sake of formality; it is generally done at the end of the project. The lessons learned process should ideally take place throughout the project, culminating in the project closure process. However, in practice, it becomes very difficult to carry out the formal lessons learned discussion before the close-out. Before the project closes out, team members are too busy and too focused working on the tasks assigned to produce the deliverables. Nevertheless, if you look at this practice closely, the project team is always on the lookout for best practices and if something does not work out, they adopt new ways. Similarly, if something works well, then they carry on with it. The PM and the team leads should keep documenting such things in a separate document earmarked for lessons learned. Thus, by the end of the project that document becomes a repository for lessons learned. A final lessons learned exercise should be performed at the end to wrap up this process and also to give it a holistic view. Regular documentation of the lessons learned ensures that points are not missed because of the long duration of the project. Many people may drop off from the project by the time the project comes to an end and, moreover, people may also forget many lessons, good or bad, as time passes. Project managers who do not document the lessons during the course of the project generally scramble around for input at the last moment. They face lot of difficulty in acquiring the quality and quantity of input that may be available if asked for at the right moment. In general, very few people are left by the end of the project and most of the team members released from the organization cannot be contacted. This makes the task of feedback collection even more challenging.

Some pundits propose to capture the lessons during project status meetings; however, you may find this impractical, the reason being that people generally do not have enough bandwidth and inclination to discuss this every week. Instead, you might schedule a dedicated monthly meeting for one hour involving leads from all functional areas. Ask the leads to collect input from their respective teams and compile them in the common lessons learned document. The documented lessons can be discussed in the meeting, along with any undocumented feedback. Some PMs schedule lessons learned meetings at the end of major project milestones or project phases. These milestones and phases are the logical transition points in the project where the team can take a deep breath, look back at what they did, how they did it—and given another chance, how they would like to do the same task in the future. The team can discuss the challenges faced, how some issues can be avoided or impacts reduced in the future, and what they did well for which they can be proud of and can repeat in the future. Look at what went right and what went wrong, and encourage the team to express their experiences. Make it clear that people should not resort to finger-pointing. Discuss the process and task rather than the people and group. To make this a planned activity, put the lessons learned task in the project schedule and estimate for it in your project budget.

Mature organizations have a central repository for storing the lessons learned contents from all the projects. Without this arrangement, it is very cumbersome and difficult to catch hold of the right kind of lessons learned from previous projects. If stored and cataloged properly, this can serve the organization in a big way. People may pull relevant information from the lessons learned database or a central site to implement the good practices and at the same time avoid the mistakes done in previous projects. Lessons learned exercises can also be used as an input into the process improvement of the project and the organization. For example, suppose a project went ahead into the user acceptance testing (UAT) without formally obtaining and documenting the user acceptance criteria and later realized that the qualities of the deliverables were way below the quality standard the users had expected. This led to a major rework requiring plenty of extra expenditures. This is a good lesson for future projects. To improve the process, a task can be added to

Item #	Action Item	Owner	Due Date	Status (Open/Close)

Figure 2.13 Lessons learned.

the WBS or the master project schedule template to obtain user acceptance criteria in the beginning of the project, say before the development work starts. Internal QA can plan and perform verification, validation, and testing—considering the acceptance criteria as the benchmark.

If your organization has a template for this document, use that template; otherwise, create one for your project. At a minimum, the document should have the project name, names and roles of people contributing to the lessons learned process, and the actual lessons learned. For the actual content of lessons learned, a tabular form works the best, one that can be divided into two parts: one for good practices and one for areas of improvement. This can further be subdivided by major task or function. For example, in a software project, the subdivision might consist of Requirements, Design, Development, Testing, Implementation, Project Management, General, etc. Another categorization can be made based on various disciplines or the aspects of the project, such as technical, cost, scope, schedule, quality, etc. The name of the person reporting the best practices and areas of improvement should be avoided. The names and roles were already cited in the beginning of the document, irrespective of who reported the lesson and who suggested what. The date of reporting can be included for the purpose of tracking the history (Figure 2.13).

Email Etiquette

Email is the most frequently used tool for written communication in the modern business world, so one must be aware of little tidbits to enhance the effectiveness and impact of communication. A message should be understood clearly when read quickly. This can be achieved if the message is well planned, simple, clear, and direct. The message should always be easy to read.

In general:

1. Know in advance what your target is.
2. Use concise language and stick to the point.

3. Use powerful and persuasive language.
4. Own the message and display confidence.

Now for a few simple do's and don'ts that can do wonders for your email communications:

Don'ts:

1. Think twice before replying to ALL because it adds to the traffic and may create communication overload.
2. Keep the signature short (maximum four or five lines); it should contain designation, department, and company name; calling numbers; and email id. Adding an email id is a good practice because sometimes the actual email id does not display in the address bar when the email is received from a different organization or from a different domain.
3. The signature should be smaller when you are replying or forwarding an email, with some exceptions based on the situation.
4. Avoid punch lines or jazzy flashy content in the signature for project-related formal emails. You might like a punch line and might strongly believe in it; however, do not use it in formal project emails.
5. The content of the email should generally be kept to just one page. If the content is very long, the use of an attachment is suggested in such a way that email has the main message and the attachment serves as an addendum, extra information, example, and supporting facts. A short message encourages the recipient to read it and read it on time, which is a very important part of effective communication.
6. Avoid the use of slang for formal communication.
7. Avoid the use of emotions.
8. The use of too many colors, fonts, and font styles should be avoided.
9. Do not put a read receipt for every email. If you think someone is ignoring your email, then only use it for records purpose. Using this feature in every email is not good practice and, moreover, adds more messages to your inbox.
10. MS Outlook provides a feature to recall the message. However, you may find that this feature is a waste, but many people still use it. If you hit the Send button prematurely, do not recall the message; instead, send another email, apologizing for the previous message and requesting receivers to ignore the previous message. When you recall the message, Outlook sends another email to the receivers instead of just making the earlier message disappear. But if you send another email apologizing for the mistake, then it will make you look better and more formal.

11. Remember that sometimes a phone call, messenger, or personal meeting works better than email. Confidential and sensitive matters should be avoided in email communications.
12. Avoid HTML pages with heavy, flashy, and colorful backgrounds.
13. Avoid typing in CAPITAL letters; it is implied as shouting and is considered rude.
14. Avoid using the High Priority option unnecessarily.
15. Avoid passive voice in your sentences.
16. Avoid using URGENT and IMPORTANT in the subject line.
17. The message should not appear offensive or rude to anyone. Pay extra attention when the message is addressed to or going to senior management. Appear polite and nice and try to provide full and complete information so that the executives may not have to follow up. You can understand the urgency that may be caused to you by even a single email that comes to you as a follow up from the senior executives. Consider the two messages below; Mark is a VP in the organization to whom you send a monthly progress report on every third day of the month copying some other executives. Report was due yesterday but you could not send it on time because you do not have all the inputs from the team since some critical members from whom you expect inputs were on vacation in past five days. So, you are notifying Mark about the delay before he inquires.

Ordinary message:

> Mark,
> Please expect a bit of delay in the progress report for the last month. Please call me if you have any question.
> Thanks,
> Shankar Jha
> Office: XXX-XXX-XXXX

Good message:

> Hello Mark
> I am in the process of acquiring inputs and validating them with the project team to ensure accuracy of the information. This might delay the distribution of the progress report by at least one more day.
> I am sorry for the delay; please let me know if you are looking for any particular information in the mean time.
> Thanks and Regards,
> Shankar Jha
> Office: XXX-XXX-XXXX

Do's:

1. Include those in "To" from whom you expect a response or to whom you are addressing the email directly.
2. Keep those in "Cc" whom you want to keep in the loop so that they are aware of the communication. Avoid the use of "Bcc" because emails have wings and you never know who can misuse the email. People whom you have kept in "To" and "Cc" may not like it when they find that someone has been blank carbon copied.
3. Subject should be relevant and should reveal the main purpose of the email.
4. The first line of the email should always address the subject of the email. Messages not related to the subject should be written last.
5. It is a good practice to address the others starting with *Hi* or *Hello*. For example, *Hi John* or *Hello John*. *Dear* can also be used to pay respect.
6. Be concise and to the point in your replies; this is not the place to showcase your essay writing skills.
7. Perform a spelling and grammar check before sending the message. If the message is going out to senior management or outside the organization, this step must be performed.
8. If the attachment is heavy, zip the file and then attach.
9. Sometimes you need to deliver different messages to different people in the same email. First addressee(s) should be the main recipient(s) of the message. Start the message for other addressees or groups of addressees on separate lines. It is a good idea to bold the name of these addressees as shown below:

> Hi Jon,
> This is in response to your voicemail. ......
> **Mary,** please provide Jon with the latest status on the progress of development work.
> **All,** please plan to update the project website with the status of your progress by noon every Friday.
> Thanks,
> Shankar Jha
> Office: XXX-XXX-XXXX

Although email is used for most project communications, one should not treat it as a formula for all situations. Conflicts can seldom be resolved through emails. This will rather escalate the issue and also waste time. Take a situation where two individuals on the project do not get along with each other and because of their personal conflict, the work is impacted. Knowing this fact, you (the PM) may not want to outrightly send them an email asking them to work together. You would like to talk to them separately first, understand their challenges and concerns, and then resolve the situation through discussion. Email should be avoided for sensitive communications. When you need information quickly from a person, you may not want to send an email because you cannot be sure if/when the other party will read the email. If the person is located nearby, you could just walk down to his/her office, or you can just call (phone) or send message through IM (Instant Messenger). Face-to-face discussion is very helpful in building rapport and understanding all aspects of a topic from the perspective of the other person. Remember that most of the time, there are no straightforward answers and solutions to any problem or any issue. So don't merely rely on email every time. You might receive a lot of helpful information by talking to people offline and understanding their perspective, which may reveal internal politics, workarounds, historical background, human connections, etc. This will help tremendously in interpersonal relationships that may further help you get the work done easily and quickly. At the same time, one must consider the amount of time that face-to-face communication demands and thus may not be possible all the time. Use phone calls, face-to-face talk, and IM for informal communications.

Often, PMs must do a lot of follow-ups to get the work done. It is never so straightforward that you prepare a project plan and a project schedule, communicate the process and timelines to everyone, and then the ball starts rolling smoothly along. Suppose a task is estimated to be completed in a week. You send an email to the concerned people on Monday to start the work, and you ask the status of the work on the following Monday, expecting that the work would have been done by that time. Under normal circumstances, you would be extremely lucky if the work is completed by then. There are so many dependencies, assumptions, and risks involved in the projects at every step that one has to assess the situation frequently and take prompt action to remove the roadblocks. They cannot always be resolved through emails. In the above example, the PM should inquire via phone call or stop by the key resources every alternate day or so, as may be appropriate, to find out how things are going, whether anyone is facing any trouble, and whether someone is waiting for something. More often than not, you will find that there are some niggles that the team would like to clear out. You (the PM) can play an important role in facilitating conversations and discussions. If you do not inquire proactively, then the information may not be available to you in time to react. Follow-up is a very important day-to-day activity in project management. But one should not confuse it with micro-management. You need not go into the gory details of the problem all the time and you need not interfere in how resources are working. At the same time, you should inquire if the work is on track and whether they are facing any kind of trouble that might impact the timelines, cost, and quality. You will find that a phone call or face-to-face conversation is better in these circumstances.

Emails are very helpful in situations where you are communicating with a customer or vendor external to your company and your organization, and where you need to keep a record of the communication for future reference. If the information is not needed right at that moment, then email is a handy communication channel to use. If the communication needs to go to a group of people, then use email; however, too many "Reply All"s may create chaos, so be careful with that and if the situation gets out of control, ask people to stop replying to the email chain and offer to have a meeting to discuss the issue. Email is best suited for general announcements and other kinds of formal communication. Suppose a very critical discussion happened over the phone and you want to keep a formal record of the communication. Follow up on the one-on-one discussion with email, stating, "As per our discussion," and then use the points of discussion or major decisions. This way, the other party will not feel offended and you will be able to keep a record of the discussion to refer back to in future.

MS Outlook offers many excellent features, such as follow-up reminders, read receipts, flagging of messages, changing the status from read to unread, archive, voting buttons, etc. If emails are archived properly into meaningful folders, that may save you a lot of time. You should never delete emails; rather, you should archive them properly. Email organization is very important for project managers and everyone else. Create one folder for every project you are handling. Every project can have sub-folders based on major functions, activities, and major applications. The use of a sub-folder for signoff is a big help in the later stages of a project. Keep all the approvals and sometimes major decisions in this folder so that you may not have to search for one or two emails in an ocean of emails. Examples of sub-folders for major functions and activities might be: KM (knowledge management), DP (defect prevention), CM (configuration management), PM (project management), and UAT (user acceptance testing). You can have a general or a non-project folder for all the general communications that are not related to the project. Create a folder for old projects and move the closed-out projects to that folder so that you do not have too many folders to handle at any one point in time. With regard to the use of voting buttons, this can be very helpful in getting a formal go/no-go decision or formal approval. You can set up the voting options while sending a decision item or attach a final deliverable and ask folks to reply using the voting buttons. Providing a link to a shared drive or a sharepoint site is better than attaching documents in the email. But make sure that recipients have access to the sharepoint or shared drive.

If you are attaching MS Word and MS Excel documents with the email, be careful about the few points as mentioned below:

1. Always check the Header and Footer. It is particularly easy to miss in MS Excel because they are not visible when you open the document in the normal screen view. If not updated properly, it might be embarrassing to you when the audience reads from the printouts and finds an inappropriate header/footer.
2. Check the Properties of the document and change organization, document name, and author name if required. This is very important when the email is going outside the organization.

3. Always do a print preview before sending out a document because many people like to read documents from printouts. Contents might appear all right
on your computer screen but might be distorted on printout. So, do a print
preview and, if required, adjust the format and setting before sending the
document.

4. Some data requires additional security and you would not like everyone
to open the document. This can be achieved by protecting the document
through password, which can be shared with only those who need to know
them. Go to Tools -> Option -> Security to set the password. This may be
required on top of the security measures and methods identified in the configuration management plan (CM plan).

There are many other good practices with regard to email and MS Outlook that
one should follow. One of them is auto-reply. For example, if you are out of the
office for a few hours in a day, or for the entire day, then set the "out-of-office" auto
reply so that senders get an auto-reply the first time they send you an email after
you set the rule. Cite your back-up for that time period and specify a phone number
where they can contact you in case of urgency. The out-of-office message should not
be very long; keep it concise yet complete. Apart from the out-of-office auto-reply
setup, mark your calendar as "Out of Office" for the period so that people can set
up meetings with you accordingly. Another good practice is to create and maintain
a distribution list for different groups that you and your team may use frequently.
This will avoid extra typing and will drastically reduce the chance of key members
getting missed in the communication process.

Microsoft® PowerPoint®

This is one of the most widely used tools for presentation so it is very important
to be aware of some useful tips to make the presentation look better and smarter.
Project managers may be required to do the presentation to the customers, senior
management, and other outside parties. Some common occasions are project kickoff meetings, exit gate reviews, project performance and status reviews with senior
management, design approach reviews, project process presentations, milestone
review presentations, lessons learned presentations, project closure presentations,
and any other ad-hoc presentations as and when needed. As a management professional, you may also be required to do the presentation outside the project duty.
There are many parts to a presentation—preparation (content collection, slide preparation, environmental set-up that includes seating arrangement, projector, light,
sound, etc.); visual aids (MS PowerPoint); verbal and nonverbal (gesture, posture,
gate up, and facial expression). A PowerPoint slide presentation is just one part of
the entire presentation package, so it should fit in nicely to play just its role without

interfering with other parts of the presentation. Following are some do's and don'ts that one should keep in mind:

1. Start the presentation with the introduction of the topic and the matter that you are going to cover in the presentation. The duration of the introduction should fit proportionately to the entire duration of the presentation.

2. Conclude with a summary of the presentation so that important points are recapped. Time should be managed properly so that the presentation does not occur in a hurry. At the same time, there should be enough time left at the end of the presentation for questions and answers.

3. Do not make the slides verbose. Provide bullet points and use smaller sentences; otherwise, the audience will become distracted and will be busy reading from the slide while you are speaking. They will neither be able to focus on reading nor on your speech. Small sentences and bullet points will need smaller spans for reading the point while you are explaining and thus the focus will be on listening rather than reading. Write phrases, not sentences.

4. Animation and slide transitions should be used consistently, if at all, for an effective presentation; otherwise use them sparingly. Sometimes it gives a nice touch when you make the text and graphics appear on-screen just when you need them. However, do not be tempted, an overdose of animation can have a distracting effect.

5. Use special effects for emphasizing a point but use them sparingly and judiciously to limit animation only to the key points. Again, animation choices should be consistent throughout the presentation.

6. You can give a professional touch to the presentation without distracting the audience by using consistent slide transitions and timings.

7. Avoid big file sizes because they may create difficulty in editing the presentation or running it smoothly. If you are inserting pictures in the presentation, use smaller file types if possible. Sometimes picture compression or native features of PowerPoint (tables, charts, etc.) might help.

8. Use WordArt sparingly.

9. Use the alignment option (Format menu) if you need to align and distribute the objects. Additionally, features like guides can be used to align and space objects. Guides can help in measuring distance and keep the positioning of elements consistent across multiple slides. Go to the View menu and select Grid and Guides. Then, in the Grid and Guides dialog box, select Display drawing guides on screen.

10. It is a good idea to insert a slide number so as to give an idea to the audience about the length of presentation.

11. Formatting a big presentation can be a headache if the right tools are not known. Use of the Masters option saves a lot of time. You can use the masters to keep slides consistent by adding graphics and formatting just once for all

the slides. Mastering the title master and slide master option is recommended for saving time, while also making the slides consistent.

12. Use charts and diagrams that emphasize your key points. This can be created from the Insert menu.

13. Be careful while trying to grab the viewer's attention. Sometimes people clutter the presentation with too many MS Clip Art objects. It is not important which picture you are including; what matters is how you use the space on the slide.

14. Sometimes there are differences between print and screen presentations. Presentations that look good on screen may not look as good when printed. Check background color, header, footer, etc. on both the print and screen.

15. In general, keep to one minute per slide. To keep the attention of the audience, it is important not to spend more than a minute per slide.

16. Keep the slides as simple as possible.

17. Use backgrounds that are neither very light nor very dark.

18. As a rule of thumb, avoid more than seven lines on a slide. However, sometimes you may be required to do a one-page presentation. That probably will become more cluttered because of too much information. But even in a one-page presentation, try to provide just the summary of information, and write one or two words instead of writing sentences so that the slide covers the required information, looks nice, and at the same time provides enough visual aid to the presenter and the audience. For example, if you want to convey that "At the current rate, actual project costs will exceed the original budget by 50 percent," the same information can be written as "EAC > 150% of BAC." Now, anyone familiar with project management concepts should understand what EAC and BAC stand for. Even if someone does not understand, you can explain the terms during the actual presentation.

19. Fonts should be easy to read.

20. Choose one font and font size for headlines and another font and font size for body text.

21. As a rule of thumb, avoid using more than three fonts.

22. Avoid using more than two levels of bullets (level 1 headings for main topics and level 2 headings for subtopics).

23. For slides containing a lot of text, choose simple backgrounds.

24. Avoid using all caps. (All caps are more difficult to read than upper and lower case type.)

25. Avoid underlining text. Instead, use italic or boldface type.

26. Ensure that everything on the slide can be seen or read.

Chapter 3

Charts, Graphs, and Diagrams

"A picture is worth a thousand words." Sometimes it is very complicated and difficult to present the facts through text. Large amounts of data can be visualized easily and quickly using diagrams. Charts, graphs, and diagrams are kind of a second language in business communication. It is very difficult to present, understand, and interpret the large volumes of numerical data and their relationship with different project parameters. Text may at times be confusing because everybody has a different style of writing and the reader may have various communication barriers. But a picture cannot be confusing; it always provides a straightforward view of the object. An audience will see and understand exactly what the presenter has portrayed, but text can be misconstrued and misunderstood. At times, you may find that even after multiple attempts at verbally explaining a topic, the audience remains confused until the presenter explains it by drawing a picture. Something that can be presented in half a page through a diagram or a chart may take five pages to explain in text and still not provide a clear-cut message. Senior management does not have time to read through the long story about every project, so the use of charts helps quickly review, analyze, and compare the progress of projects and their status.

It is very important for a project manager (PM) to understand various kinds of tools under this category and master them through practice. There are hundreds of tools available for general use; this book describes only the necessary and sufficient charts, graphs, and diagrams useful to a project manager. Some of these tools are used in the planning process, some in execution, while most are utilized in monitoring and control processes. This chapter explains how sometimes a single tool, with or without variation, can be used in all the project processes; for example, a Gantt chart is used in initiation, planning, execution, monitoring and control, and closure processes. There are also examples where single raw data is presented through various tools to provide different perspectives and to facilitate analysis and decision making under different circumstances.

Gantt Chart

The Gantt chart is a popular project management tool, a type of bar chart that illustrates project schedule. There are plenty of scheduling tools and the schedule can be created in a number of ways, but Gantt charts are simple to understand and easy to create. On small projects, the Gantt chart may be the only form of schedule. Because of the simple pictorial view, one can quickly understand the schedule and analyze the project scheduling problems. One can find answers to the following questions pretty quickly with a single glance at a Gantt chart:

1. When does the work start?
2. What activities are involved in finishing the entire work?
3. What is the order of activities and tasks?
4. How many people are working on each activity, and what are their names?
5. How much are the individual activities complete?
6. How many activities are complete, how many are in progress, and how many activities are yet to start?
7. How many activities finished ahead of time, how many finished late, and which activities have been delayed?
8. When is the entire work expected to finish?

Depending on the needs of the stakeholder, the Gantt chart can be customized to present only that information which is needed by the stakeholder. Customizing the view is very easy in a Gantt chart if you are preparing it with the help of MS Project. Project managers can use the Gantt chart for the purpose of analyzing the effect of various parameters affecting the project schedule. They can change the resource assignments, predecessor, successor, float, etc. to find out how the overall schedule is impacted. This analysis can help in decision making by finding alternatives to resolve resource conflicts and other project problems. These kinds of changes can be made in the Gantt chart on-the-fly to determine the overall effect. Some real-life examples are discussed later in this chapter to illustrate the communication power and effectiveness of a Gantt chart.

In a Gantt chart, each task or activity takes up one row. Dates go along the top in increments of days, weeks, months, or quarter, depending on the total length of the project. The expected time for each task is represented by a horizontal bar, where the left end marks the expected start date of the task and right end marks the expected finish date. These task elements (detail and summary) comprise the work breakdown structure of the project. Tasks may run sequentially, in parallel, or overlapping. So, Gantt charts can also be used to show the dependency (i.e., precedence network) relationships between activities. Dependency gives an idea about the order in which tasks need to be executed.

Gantt charts can be used in many different ways to provide information on various details. The first time it is plotted in the *planning process* that represents the timing of major tasks required to complete a project and the order in which they should be executed. Later, as the project progresses, they are updated during the *execution and monitoring and control* process by filling in the bars to a length proportional to the fraction of work that has been accomplished on the task. This gives an idea of what should have been achieved versus how much has been achieved. At this time, some tasks may not be required so they are dropped or a new task might have to be added.

Take a case in which you are managing a group of small to medium-sized projects that depend on each other. You have been asked to present to upper management the status of the current schedule and the plans for completing the projects. You can use percent-complete shadings and a vertical "TODAY" line to show current schedule status as shown in the example below. Current tasks that cross the "TODAY" line are behind schedule if their filled-in section is to the left of the "TODAY" line and are ahead of schedule if the filled-in section stops to the right of the "TODAY" line. Future tasks lie completely to the right of the line. This gives quick information on what should have been achieved at a point in time versus what has been completed. This is very effective in presenting both project progress and schedule status to senior management/executives. One should keep in mind that senior management's time is very precious so the chart should show the major milestones with special emphasis on critical-path tasks and those at serious risk. The example in Figure 3.1 shows timelines and the progress of all the projects planned under your program for year 2008. Notice that "Project 5" is in red because it could not start on time.

When a project is underway, Gantt charts help to monitor whether or not the project is on schedule. If it is not, a Gantt chart can be used to find the remedial action to bring the project schedule back on track. Consider the project depicted in the Gantt chart shown in Figure 3.2. Major milestones are Requirements, Design, Construction, Quality Assurance, User Acceptance Test, and Implementation. The project started in January and is planned to finish in August. Project status is monitored in mid-April and it is observed that Design is lagging behind; and at the current rate, it will not be finished on time. Because the remaining tasks are also sequential, the project will ultimately be delayed. By looking at the Gantt chart, the project manager has a few options to bring the project on course:

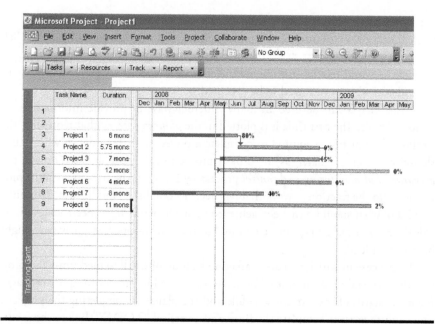

Figure 3.1 Example shows timelines and progress of all projects planned under program for year 2008.

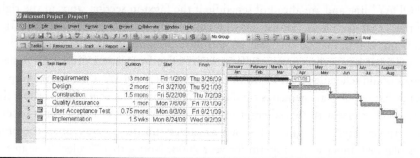

Figure 3.2 Example Gantt chart.

1. Increase the resources or replace the existing resource with more efficient resources in the Design and Development task so that it finishes on time. But, if this is not possible, then try other options.
2. Overlap quality assurance and user acceptance test tasks so that the user acceptance test finishes on time and thus the implementation is not delayed. Both options have risks involved in them so it will be a management decision in consultation with the project manager about which course to take.

In yet another example shown in Figure 3.3, the original baseline and revised baseline schedules are plotted very effectively, showing the reason for the change

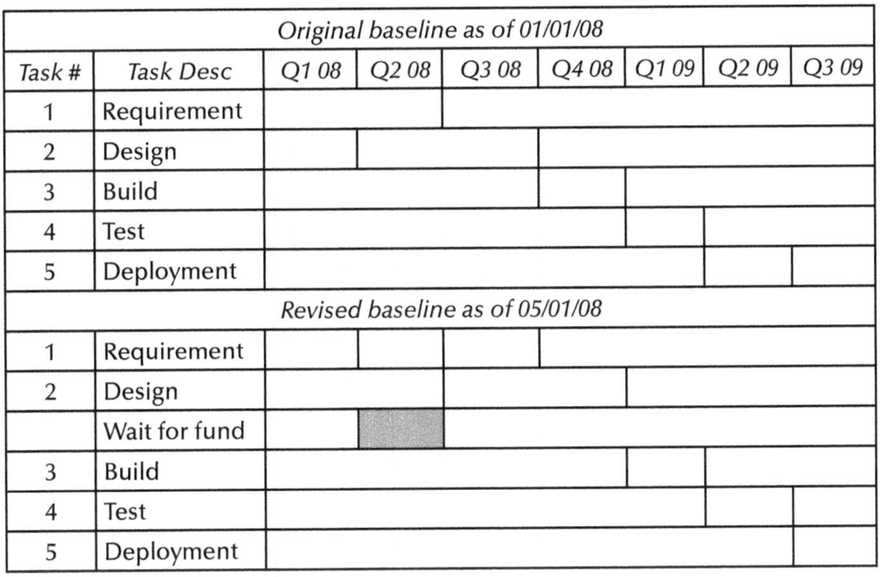

Original baseline as of 01/01/08								
Task #	Task Desc	Q1 08	Q2 08	Q3 08	Q4 08	Q1 09	Q2 09	Q3 09
1	Requirement							
2	Design							
3	Build							
4	Test							
5	Deployment							
Revised baseline as of 05/01/08								
1	Requirement							
2	Design							
	Wait for fund							
3	Build							
4	Test							
5	Deployment							

Figure 3.3   Example Gantt chart.

in schedule. Work was put on hold in Quarter 2 because funds were diverted to other strategic projects in the portfolio and no funds were available for this project. This can be plotted very easily using MS Project; alternatively, MS Excel can also be tried. The example in Figure 3.3 is depicted with the help of MS Excel; however, MS Project looks cleaner and better, and offers more features.

Now consider another situation in which you are managing a very critical project, and a particular task or phase is facing serious issues that are causing delays in finishing that task/phase and so the project is in YELLOW status. The situation is very bad, so you (the project manager) must present to senior management a plan for recovery. Senior management has asked you to bring the project plans to the meeting. You may be wondering whether you should present them the actual project management plan, the twenty-page detailed project schedule, or how should you go about it? The situation might be more frightening if you are facing such a group for the first time for this kind of crisis. There is no need to worry because a simple Gantt chart can save the day. In situations like this, list all the issues or defects and plot the time frames in which they need to be fixed or can be fixed in order to complete the phase/task. Make sure to also list the owner of each task. This will provide management with a lot of confidence about when and how the issue/defect will be fixed. The chart gives an idea of what needs to be done to get out of trouble and how the activities are lined up each day to get this done, as shown in the example in Figure 3.4. Keep the tasks to a manageable number (no more than fifteen or twenty) so that the chart

Task #	Task Desc	Owner	12-May	13-May	14-May	15-May	16-May	19-May	20-May
1	Defect 1	Jack							
2	Defect 2	Jill							
3	Defect 3	Jim							
4	Defect 4	John							
5	Defect 5	Jack							
6	Defect 6	Jill							

Figure 3.4   Example Gantt chart.

fits on a single page. More complex projects may require subordinate charts that detail the timing of all the subtasks that make up one of the main tasks.

Flowchart

As the name suggests, this is a chart that illustrates the flow of the process, data, system, and work (Figure 3.5). The tool graphically depicts the steps required to perform a task. Complex system and process interactions can be easily presented using flowcharts. It is very difficult to explain and understand such complex system interactions using text. A flowchart is a wonderful visual presentation tool and is used as an effective communication tool on the project at various stages. The best part of this tool is that everyone can create and understand the flowchart without undergoing any kind of training. As a good practice, project managers should create a simplistic view of the high-level process flow diagram in the beginning of the project to show what the project is all about. Discuss the diagram at the occasion of project kickoff. This provides a common understanding among the stakeholders. When discussed with all the stakeholders together in one meeting, it prevents costly misunderstandings at a later stage. This high-level flowchart should show the current state and how the end state will appear after the project is implemented. Stakeholders can revisit the flow diagram whenever there is any confusion. This must contain major inputs, processes, outputs, and flow. Project managers can plot it themselves or can employ the help of subject matter experts (SMEs).

A flowchart can be easily created using MS Visio and, often, simple diagrams are plotted using the features of MS Word. A flowchart can also be timelined using

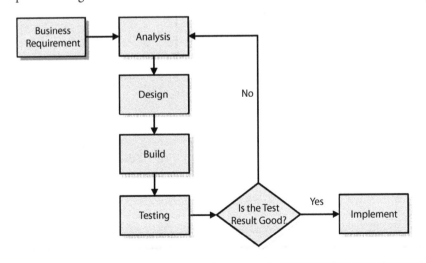

Figure 3.5 Example flowchart.

swim lanes to show the sequence of events. Flowcharts in swim lanes can be used very effectively to compare two or more processes. Another good use of swim lanes is to indicate the owner of the process step; the owner can be specified as an individual, a functional department, or an organization. These are also called cross-functional flowcharts. The advantage of this mapping approach is that a process flow that changes "lanes" indicates hand-offs. This is where a lack of coordination can cause communication problems. It also shows who oversees each part of the process. Sometimes, different phases of a process can be shown through swim lanes and the owner can be identified using a color code. The example in Figure 3.6 illustrates the flow through timeline vertical swim lanes to show a simple view of different phases of the software development life cycle of an organization. Swim lanes can be horizontal (Figure 3.7) or vertical.

Following are some common usages of the flowchart in a project:

1. Situations where you need to explain to the team the steps needed to complete a task.
2. Design and architectural approach.

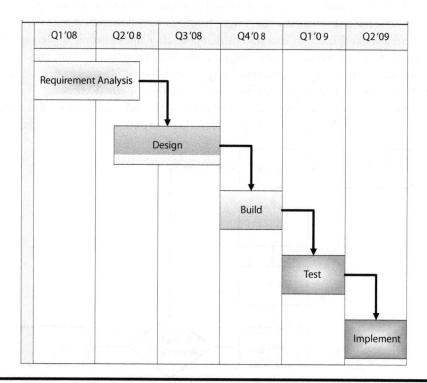

Figure 3.6 High-level plan for project XYZ.

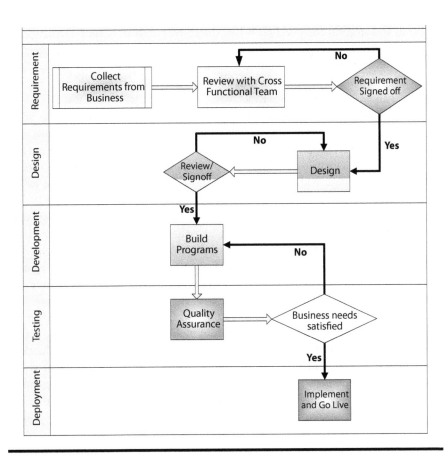

Figure 3.7   SDLC for organization ABC.

3. Organization chart: Also a kind of flowchart only. This is explained later in this chapter.
4. Scheduling charts: A simple high-level schedule can be easily and very effectively presented using a flowchart. Some examples are shown later in this chapter.
5. Logic charts to analyze a situation for problem resolution.

S Curve

The S curve is a widely used tool in projects to present cost baseline, actual cumulative cost, and a comparison of the two against time. Cumulative values of actual cost (AC), earned value (EV), planned value (PV), and budget at completion (BAC), when plotted against time, all form the shape of an "S" (flat in the beginning and end, and steep in the middle). When the above parameters are plotted against time, they provide management with various critical information on project performance, such as scope, cost (or resources), and schedule, in one graph. This can also be used for cost variance, funding requirements, and forecasting purposes. So, the S curve is an extremely powerful tool.

There are some software scheduling/project management packages that automatically generate S curves, but many scheduling/project management tools may not have this feature. MS Excel can be used to plot the cumulative values against the time/project phase using a smooth line curve as shown in Figure 3.8. MS Project has the capability of providing earned value (EV) data for a project; once the values are obtained, plot them on an MS Excel.

The cost baseline is a time-phased budget of a project; so when the cumulative cost is plotted against time, it gives the cost baseline. One can determine the budgeted cost of the project at various points and can easily forecast the budget. The chart in Figure 3.8 is a simple chart that shows the actual cumulative cost against the cost baseline. This has been plotted against the project phase so that one can view the health of the project in terms of cost at the end of the build phase. The budgeted cost at the end of build is $800,000, which is the cumulative budget for the initiation, requirements, design, and build phases. The total spent at the end of the build phase is $1,000,000, which is the cumulative actual cost of the initiation, requirements, design, and build phases. The chart clearly reveals the trend of actual cost and if the trend continues, then one can forecast the actual cost at the end of the project. The project team can figure out the cost variance and analyze the causes responsible for those variances. Based on the situation, there are a couple of options:

1. Find out creative ways to reduce the actual cost going forward so that the project remains on budget at the end without affecting other project parameters. Document the decision, make changes to the plan, and communicate to the project team and other stakeholders.
2. Alternatively, the project budget can be revised after re-estimating the remaining part of the project and by subsequent approval of the change control.

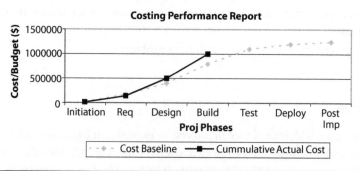

Figure 3.8 S curve.

A similar simple graph can be plotted against time (monthly, quarterly, etc.). To get a composite view of the performance, one can plot the cumulative values of PV, EV, and AC. The endpoint of PV is the value for BAC. This is called *earned value technique* (EVT).

The S curve reveals another very interesting fact: the rate of cost increase is slow in the beginning as the project starts off with just a few members. The requirements gathering phase typically has a very small number of resources. Slowly, the project gets staffed with all the core team members. Once analysis gathers momentum, a few more human resources and other resources (material and other supplies) are added. After the requirements are finalized, more hands and capital are needed in the design phase. The project reaches its peak in the build phase when the maximum amount of work takes place. There is a sudden growth in the number of human resources and amounts of other resources required to carry out the development work. Development team members start getting released in the Quality Testing phase. This is where the growth rate goes over the hump and finally flattens out because there are very few human resource and capital changes during the final phases of the project.

Column Chart

A column chart is useful for plotting a trend and for plotting comparisons. When plotted for comparison, one can use different colors for different items. This is also called a *bar chart* and sometimes a *histogram*. Histograms are a special type of bar chart used to summarize groups of data. Project managers monitor actual project cost and have to compare it with the project budget. The budget can be distributed over time and thus can be compared using this tool very effectively month by month, or quarter by quarter. The column chart is a very good tool for tracking, monitoring, and reporting resource data as illustrated in the next section ("Resource Histogram"). This is a very helpful tool for reporting purposes because it captures so much information and yet it is easy to plot, understand, and comprehend.

Following is just one example, but you can master different variations and charting functions through online help by clicking on the Help Menu in MS Excel and then clicking on Microsoft Excel Help. One of the variations is the *stacked column chart*, which can be used for showing the contribution of different components at different locations or at different times; see Figure 3.9. Another example could be a combination chart, where you can show a column chart in combination with a line chart, as later plotted in a Pareto chart.

This example is that of a software development project where the actual costs of different human resource types are compared quarter by quarter (Figure 3.9). The use of a color code makes the visual presentation strong, as it is easy to figure out the differences at a glance. One can understand how different types of resources were engaged in the project: initially, more BAs were required, but the need for this

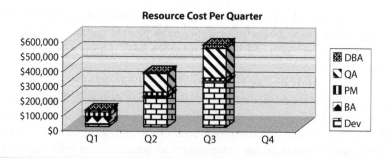

Figure 3.9   Example column chart for software development project.

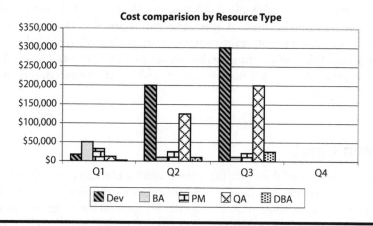

Figure 3.10   Example column chart for cost comparison by resource type.

type of resource decreased significantly and the need for development resources increased in Q2 and Q3.

The same data can be presented in a different way as shown in Figure 3.10.

Resource Histogram

The resource histogram is used for the staffing management plan; human resources are charted in the form of a bar chart or histogram. The chart illustrates the number of hours that a person, department, or entire project team will be needed each week or month over the course of the project. This chart can include a horizontal line (as shown by the 100% line in Figure 3.11) that includes the maximum number of hours available from a particular resource. Bars that extend beyond the line indicate the need for resource leveling—for example, adding more resources or extending the schedule of the project or the particular task. MS Project provides this graph automatically; go to Resource Graph from the View menu. There are several options available in Resource

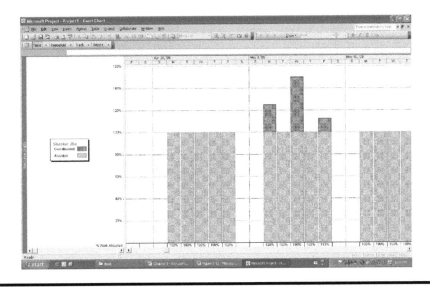

Figure 3.11   Allocation percent for resource "Shankar Jha."

Graph view: one can find out remaining availability, percentage allocation, over allocation, etc. One can set a different color for over-allocation. Figure 3.11 shows allocation percent for resource "Shankar Jha," and Figure 3.12 shows the number of over-allocated hours for the same resource for the same duration. Likewise, one can change options in MS Project to get a histogram on different parameters for the resource.

This tool is capable of producing many wonderful reports for analysis and decision-making purposes. Apart from the project manager, functional resource managers can use this tool to achieve resource leveling, efficient resource allocation, and optimum resource utilization. The powerful visual presentation of the tool makes it easy to use and analyze. One can plot week-by-week or month-by-month graphs, comparing the allocated work hours for various resources. The graph can also be plotted using MS Excel as shown in Figure 3.13. Any allocation above the 160 hours line needs to be readjusted through the resource leveling exercise. In a similar fashion, allocation versus utilization can be plotted for resources, and they can be analyzed before making adjustments.

The resource histogram is very helpful when resource managers, project managers, and program managers perform enterprise resource planning or allocate resources across multiple projects in a program. Resource allocation should be reviewed once a week or once every two weeks to make sure that no resource is over-allocated or under-allocated. They can also plot the actual efforts to review the report for over-utilization and under-utilization. Allocation and utilization can be corrected by reallocation of resources. This exercise may need input from the resource managers and all the project managers for whom the resources are working.

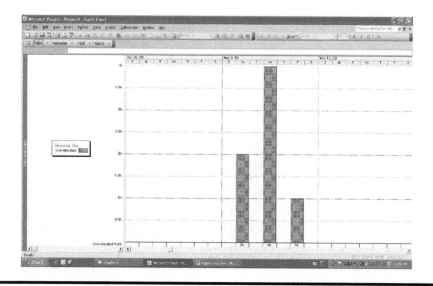

Figure 3.12 Number of over-allocated hours for the same resource for the same duration as in Figure 3.13

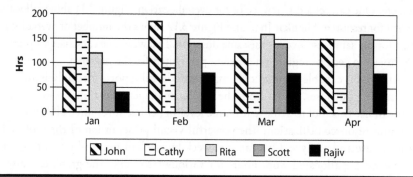

Figure 3.13 Example resource histogram.

Run Chart

Run charts are often used for quality management, but can also be used for other purposes. A run chart is also called a *line chart* or *run-sequence plot* and is used to display process performance over time. Process results or performance outcomes are plotted in chronological order against time. When data points are plotted against time and are connected by a line, they indicate a trend. Upward and downward trends, cycles, and large aberrations may be spotted and investigated further. When multiple variables are tracked on a single chart through multiple lines, with each variable having its own line, the chart is then called a multiple run chart. Keep the following points in mind while interpreting a run chart:

1. Look at the data for a long enough period of time so that a "usual" range of variation is evident. This will tell whether the improvement in result is temporary or it follows a pattern.
2. Is the recent data within the usual range of variation?
3. Look for a pattern. Is there a daily pattern? Weekly? Monthly? Yearly?

Follow the steps mentioned below to plot a run chart. It is very easy to plot using MS Excel.

1. Collect a set of fifteen or more data points.
2. Show events and values on the y-axis after determining the scale for values.
3. Mark the time (day, month, quarter, etc.) on the x-axis.
4. Plot the data values in the sequence in which they occurred.
5. Draw lines to connect the points on the graph.
6. Calculate the average of the data points. Usually, an average line is added to a run chart to clarify movement of the data away from the average. An average line runs parallel to the x-axis. In cases where the data points are asymmetrical, use the median instead of the mean. The median is calculated as the average of the highest and the lowest values or the data point in the middle of the highest and the lowest values. For the sake of distinction, color the average line differently.
7. Circle the point and annotate the chart where the process was changed to show the improvement in result because of the process change. In the example in Figure 3.14, the process change could be the inclusion of an internal review process before the product is released to the quality assurance/control team.

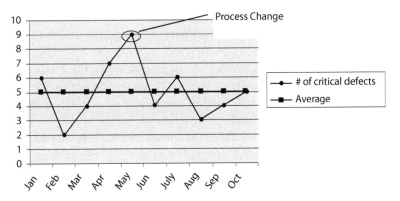

Figure 3.14   Run chart.

Pareto Chart

The Pareto chart is a very good tool for problem analysis, cost analysis, and decision making. The tool is widely used and easily understood. This is a very common and basic tool for quality control. A Pareto chart is also known as a *Pareto diagram*, which is used to separate the vital few from trivial many. It works on the principle that when several factors affect a situation, a few factors account for most of the impact. So, the tool is useful when there are many problems or causes and one wants to focus on the most significant and the most dominant ones. The example presented at the end of this topic provides a very good illustration of how and when this tool can be used. Use this tool for setting priorities so that available limited resources can be aligned and organized to achieve the maximum returns. The Pareto chart organizes data in such a way that makes the relative importance of the categories of data apparent to the user. Precaution must be taken while using this tool—always use objective data instead of opinions and votes.

A Pareto chart is a bar graph. The lengths of the bars represent frequency, cost, time, or money and are arranged with longest bars to the left and the shortest bars to the right. In general, the left-hand-side vertical axis represents the frequency, cost, or other important measure and the right-hand-side vertical axis represents cumulative frequency, total cost, or total of any such measurement. The horizontal axis represents categories or groups. Follow the steps below to plot the chart:

1. First of all, list all the problems and group them. Determine the categories to be used for grouping items.
2. Determine the appropriate measurement of the problem. Common measurements are frequency (how often a problem occurs), quantity (how much is required to finish the job), cost (how many resources are needed), and time (how long it takes).
3. Determine the time period the Pareto chart will cover (e.g., one work cycle, one full day, a week, etc.).
4. Collect frequency data for each category or group. Do a subtotal for each group.
5. To plot the bar chart, determine an appropriate scale. The maximum value will be the largest subtotal from Step 4. (If you will do optional Steps 7 and 8 below, the maximum value will be the sum of all subtotals from Step 4.) Mark the scale on the left side of the chart.
6. Draw bars for each group. Place the group with highest frequency (tallest bar) at the far left, then the next tallest to its right, etc. If there are many groups with small measurements, they can be grouped as "Miscellaneous" or "Other."

Steps 7, 8, and 9 are optional but are useful for analysis and communication.

7. Compute the percentage for each group as a subtotal for that group divided by the total for all categories. Draw a right vertical axis and label it with percentages. Make sure that the two scales match; for example, the left measurement that corresponds to one-half should be exactly opposite "50%" on the right scale.

8. Compute cumulative sums and draw. Add the subtotals for the first and second groups and place a dot above the second bar indicating that sum. To that sum add the subtotal for the third group, and place a dot above the third bar for that new sum. Continue the process for all the bars. Connect the dots, starting at the top of the first bar. The last dot should reach "100%" on the right scale.

9. Draw a horizontal line at the "80%" mark and drop a vertical line from the point the horizontal "80%" line touches the curve. Categories present on the left-hand side of the vertical line represent vital few and those on the other side are trivial many. This is called the 80/20 rule, meaning that 80 percent of the defects or problems are caused by 20 percent of all the contributing factors. So, one should focus on the vital 20 percent of the causes.

The chart in Figure 3.15 was created using the "Line – Column on 2 Axes" graph option in MS Excel. To draw the 80/20 line, copy the graph into MS Paint, draw the line, and copy the graph from Paint back to your presentation.

There may be many different causes for defects in a project. These defects are grouped appropriately. Causes responsible for an insignificant number of defects are grouped together in the "Others" category. The chart gives management or a project team a message that most of the defects (80 percent) will be fixed if the root causes for "Unskilled Resource" and "Oversight" are removed. Instead of devising methods for preventing (not fixing) the defects randomly or in the order they were detected, one should focus on removing the significant causes. There is always a mismatch between the number of issues and the resource and budget available for the project. So, to make the best use of time, resources, and budget to achieve maximum

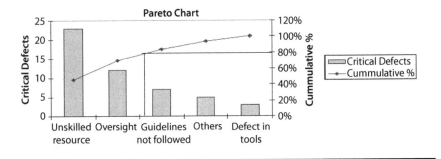

Figure 3.15 Pareto chart.

benefit, one should carry out this exercise and then engage the resources appropriately. Senior management approval must be obtained regarding which group should be targeted first, before engaging resources, because sometimes there may be other considerations not so apparent to the project manager. Use brainstorming and the cause and effect diagram for finding the root causes. Once the root cause is known, then follow the PDCA (Plan Do Check Act) process to fix the problem.

Cause-and-Effect Diagram

Also known as the Ishikawa diagram or fishbone diagram, this tool is used primarily for quality control processes. As the name suggests, the tool helps in systematically finding all the root causes leading to a single effect. For plotting a cause and effect diagram, use MS Visio, which has a template for this diagram under Business Process category. The diagram looks exactly like a fish bone skeleton and thus derives its name, the fishbone diagram. The process of drawing the fishbone is a very good way to involve team members and subject matter experts to solicit their opinion and capture the suggestions systematically to resolve the problem. When team members are involved, they have the feeling of being part of the project and being important to the project. At the same time, when they provide an opinion or suggest something, they will show ownership of the idea and thus it will be easier to implement solutions.

From the previous example used in the Pareto chart in Figure 3.15, "Unskilled Resource" is the major contributor to project defects, so one must try to minimize this factor. A root cause analysis can be done as shown in Figure 3.16 to find out roots of the problem and they can be tackled one by one or together through a process improvement plan. The problem or the issue (for example, "unskilled resource") forms the head of the central arrow. Based on the type of industry and nature of the project, causes can be categorized suitably into categories, such as M's (Man, Machine, Material, Method, etc,) and P's (People, Process, Plant/Place, Policies, Product, etc.). Next, root causes as agreed to by the team are added to each category. Subject matter experts, team leads, and the PM brainstorm to determine the root cause for every category. Thereafter, the process improvement can be planned and implemented for the root causes. For example, to tackle "Low interest for training," training can be made mandatory for every team member by allocating this as a task in the project schedule and allocating time for it. Additionally, it can be added as a task in the employee appraisal system to encourage employees and make them interested. Apart from other things, employees can be rewarded and be given incentives based on the training they perform. Other solutions could be the availability of better, livelier training material and the use of good professional trainers. The root causes can be listed in order from most likely and most important to least likely and least important. This will give the team an idea as to the order in which they should

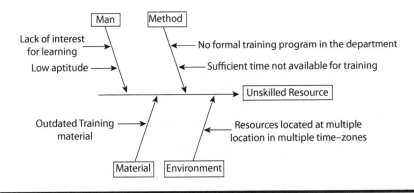

Figure 3.16 Cause and effect diagram.

be working. As described in this example, a lack of interest for learning is caused by insufficient time available for training and outdated training material. So, these three root causes can be tackled as a single cause for removing most of the instances of unskilled resource. Sometimes, a single root cause can be associated with more than one category. Those repeating causes should be given top priority. The PM needs to make such decisions often with the help of the team members.

Pie Chart

As the name suggests, the pie chart looks like a pie and is circular in shape. The chart appears as if the pie has been sliced into many parts. This statistical chart is used to show the contribution of individual elements to the total. Classes or groups of data are shown in proportion to the whole data set. The entire pie represents all the data, while each slice or sector represents a different class or group within the whole. The length of each arc (in the case of a two-dimensional chart) or the area of each sector (in the case of a three-dimensional chart) is equal the proportion it represents compared to the entire data set. The use of color provides an enhanced visual presentation. There are many options available in MS Excel, so create a chart based on the specific need for better visual presentation.

Use the tool when it is necessary to compare the size of a slice with that of the whole pie, rather than comparing the slices among them. Pie charts work particularly well when the slices represent 25 or 50 percent of the data, but in general, other plots such as the bar chart, dot plot, or a nongraphical method such as a table may be more appropriate for representing the information.

It is difficult to compare different sections of a given pie chart, or to compare data across different pie charts. It is not recommended to use a pie chart when you have to compare slices with one another; the bar chart is preferable in such situations. Use this chart to show cost distribution, defect distribution, etc.

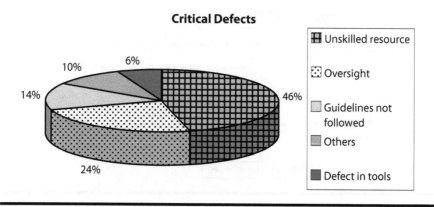

Figure 3.17 Example pie chart.

A pie chart can be plotted and formatted very easily in MS Excel. In the two examples in Figure 3.17 and Figure 3.18, one shows percentage while the other shows absolute value. One graph is three-dimensional (Figure 3.17) while the other is a two-dimensional (Figure 3.18) chart. The charts can be modified based on the need and the situation to make it more suitable and better for visual presentation.

Control Chart

The control chart is a very powerful, yet cryptic and complex statistical process control tool. Project managers may not use this very often for one particular project, but this tool will be quite helpful in managing the program or portfolio. There are multiple varieties of this tool, as described later, which are applicable to different

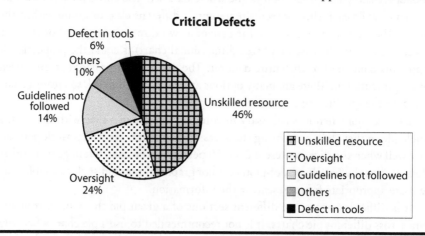

Figure 3.18 Example pie chart.

situations. The control chart is used to verify process stability. Process stability is very important in any process improvement initiative. Programs and projects use many processes to bring order, predictability, and consistency in the delivery of intermediate as well as final products and services. Results should be tracked over time using a suitable control chart to distinguish special causes of variation from common causes of variation and to study how a process changes over time.

Following are the characteristics of a stable process:

1. All causes of variation are known.
2. Variations are acted upon.
3. The process is governed by the common causes of variation.
4. The output of the process is predictable to a great extent.

Following are the situations when a control chart should be used:

1. Controlling ongoing processes by finding and correcting problems as they occur
2. Predicting the expected range of outcomes from a process
3. Determining whether a process is stable (in statistical control)
4. Analyzing patterns of process variation from special causes (non-routine events) or common causes (built into the process)
5. Determining whether your quality improvement project should aim to prevent specific problems or to make fundamental changes to the process

It is important to understand the concept of common and special causes of variation:

Common cause: These are the causes of variation built in the process itself. They cannot be easily eliminated without significant investment in terms of cost, time, etc. These are the fluctuations in the process output caused by unknown factors that result in *steady but random* distribution of output around the average line. Common cause provides a measure of the process potential; in other words, it tells how well the process would perform in the absence of special causes of variation. Common cause of variation is also known as random variation, noise, uncontrollable variation, within-group variation, or inherent variation. Some examples of common causes are mentioned below:
1. Poor working condition (e.g., imagine a worker working in an underground coal mine where there is insufficient lighting, improper ventilation, a hot and humid environment, air pollution, etc.) Working conditions cannot be improved without significant investment.
2. Poor design
3. Substandard raw material
4. Inappropriate procedure

5. Incompetent workforce
6. Variability in settings
7. Poor machine maintenance

Special cause: These are caused because of a particular problem that is unanticipated, new, or previously neglected phenomena within the system. This kind of variation is *unpredictable* and always arrives as a surprise. Variations due to these causes can be easily identified and eliminated. Examples of special cause are:

1. Lack of technical skills
2. Lack of domain knowledge
3. Non-availability of the right kind of infrastructure
4. Wrong design
5. Process change
6. Poor batch of raw material
7. Computer crash
8. Sudden unplanned vacations by a large percentage of the workforce

There are two more very important concepts that one should understand before learning the types of control charts. Data can be categorized in two types:

■ *Variable data:* Anything measurable is called variable data. It is also called *quantitative* data. Variable data is measured in quantitative units. This should answer the question of "how much?"; examples include effort deviation, percent schedule variation, weight, etc.
■ *Attribute data:* Attribute data is nonmeasurable data and it is the lowest level of data. It is purely binary in nature. Good or Bad; Yes or No. Attribute data is *qualitative* data that can be counted for recording and analysis. This should answer the question of "how many?"; examples include number of defects in a batch, the presence or absence of a required label, bug fixes accepted or rejected, etc.

A control chart always has a central line for the average, an upper line for the *upper control limit* (UCL), and a lower line for the *lower control limit (LCL)*. These lines are determined from historical data. By comparing current data to these lines, you can draw conclusions about whether the process variation is consistent (in control) or is unpredictable (out of control, affected by special causes of variation).

Control charts for variable data are *used in pairs*. The top chart monitors the average, or the centering of the distribution of data from the process. The bottom chart monitors the range, or the width of the distribution. Control charts for attribute data are used as a *single chart*. There are various types of control charts available for both these types of data; some of them are listed below.

1. *Attribute data:*
   - P chart: Also referred as fraction of defective.
   - Np chart: Shows number of defective items. The Np chart is used when the size of the subgroup (N) is constant; the P chart is used when it is not constant.
   - C chart: C stands for count (e.g., count of defectives per lot).
   - U chart: It is similar to a C chart, the difference being, C chart is used when the material being measured is constant in area and every subgroup has equal size. The U chart is used when either one of these assumptions is not valid.
2. *Variable data:*
   - I-MR chart: If the measurement is costlier or a destructive testing is involved, this chart can be used to monitor the process. Here the sample size is 1 for individual chart and it is 2 for moving range chart.
   - Xbar/R chart: When the sample size is between 2 and 15, average and range chart can be used to monitor and control the process. Here, X represents the individual value, Xbar represents the mean or average, and R represents range.

One can use a decision tree or some kind of matrix as shown in Figure 3.19 to identify the type of control chart needed for the data. Here, the data column refers to the number of measurements in each group or subgroup. You may find differences in various reference materials as far as the count of the data column goes into determining the type of chart; so again, go by the standard your organization has set for itself or as the situation demands.

The overall basic procedure for plotting and using the control chart is as follows:

Data Columns	Data	Chart
1	Integers (attribute)	C chart
2	Integers (constant sample)	Np chart
2	Integers (varying sample)	P or U chart
1	Decimals (variable)	XmR chart (Individuals and Moving Range)
2-10	Decimals or integers	Xbar R chart (Average and Range)
10+	Decimals or integers	Xbar S chart (Average and Standard Deviation)

Figure 3.19   Control chart decision matrix.

1. Select the appropriate control chart based on the type of data.
2. Determine the appropriate time period for collecting and plotting the data.
3. Collect the data, construct the chart, and analyze the data.
4. Find the "out-of-control indicators" on the control chart. When one is identified, mark it on the chart and investigate the cause. Document how you investigated, what you learned, the cause, and how it was corrected.
5. Continue to plot data as it is generated. As each new data point is plotted, check for new out-of-control signals.
6. When you start a new control chart, the process may be out of control. If so, the control limits calculated from the first 20 points are conditional limits. When you have at least twenty sequential points from a period when the process is operating in control, recalculate the control limits.

How to Interpret Out-of-Control Indicators

Following are the signals of special cause of variation. The process is said to be "Not in Control"/"Not stable" when any one or more signals appear in the chart. You may find variations in the following rule in different reference materials, so follow the one recognized by your organization and authorized by your quality assurance team.

1. A single point outside the UCL or LCL.
2. Two of three successive points are on the same side of the centerline and farther than 2σ from it.
3. Five successive points are on the same side of the centerline and farther than 1σ from it.
4. A run of eight in a row is on the same side of the centerline, or 10 out of 11, 12 out of 14, or 16 out of 20.
5. Obvious consistent or persistent patterns that suggest something unusual about your data and your process. Watch out for random patterns such as trends, cycles, or an unusual spread of points within the control limits.

The control chart in Figure 3.20 has three sections. The first section shows one point outside the UCL. This indicates that a source of special cause of variation is present, and needs to be analyzed and resolved. Data points outside the control limits are easily noticeable. For the purpose of analysis, highlight that point and determine the reason for variance. For example, suppose that in a particular month during software development, there was a spike in coding defects that led to the variance. This may be due to having too many unskilled developers working on the code and somehow the defect prevention tools were not effectively utilized.

The process appears to be in control in the second section of the control chart in Figure 3.20. However, it is not really a smooth flowing process. All

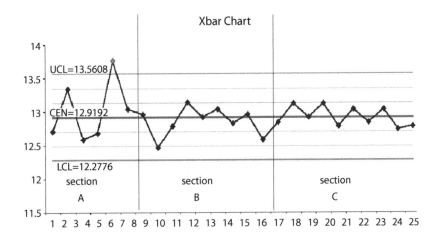

Figure 3.20 Control chart.

the points lie within the control limits and thus exhibit only common cause variations.

In section C in Figure 3.20, notice that the trend is more predictable and flows smoothly. This section proves that the process improvement has worked, the process is now stable, and future performance of the process is predictable.

Therefore, to summarize, eliminating special causes of variation keeps the process in control; process improvement reduces the process variation and moves the control limits in toward the centerline of the process. At the beginning of this process run, it was in need of adjustment as the product output was sporadic. An adjustment was made, and while the plotted points were now within the boundaries, it was still not centered on the process specification. Finally, the process was tweaked a little more and in the third section, the process seems to center around the average line.

Note that UCL and LCL are not specification limits. Control limits are calculated based on process performance. *Specification limits* are based on customer or organization requirements. One must secure the templates of these charts from the organizational process asset or some other dependable source. Building one from the scratch requires extensive knowledge and practice of the concepts of statistical process control and, in particular, the control chart.

Organization Chart

The organization chart (Figure 3.21) is a very useful communication tool that helps stakeholders understand the organizational hierarchy, escalation levels, and communication path. This chart allows team members, customers, and senior

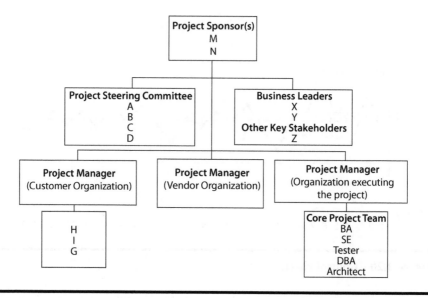

Figure 3.21 Organization chart.

management to understand who is working on the project and what their roles are. A project organization chart is different from a company's organization chart. The nature of project organization is temporary and dynamic. A complete chart should not only show the organization of the project team, but also the organization of the project governing body, steering committee, key customer's organization, vendor organization, and the organization of any other team with which the project interacts. If the diagram becomes too complicated and big, it can be broken down into smaller diagrams. Use MS Visio to draw this chart. MS Visio provides an excellent feature for showing teams separately with the help of dotted rectangular frames. Sometimes, color coding is used to identify and show different teams. The chart is hierarchical in structure, so it starts with the higher or senior level and branches downward to the most junior level. A solid line shows a direct relationship between superior and the subordinate. Indirect reporting or relationship is generally shown with the help of dotted arrow.

The project organization chart avoids confusion and saves time for team members because once the team members understand the roles and organization structure, they approach the right person for the right kind of job and information. This essentially helps on bigger projects where multiple organizations are involved and where the team size is very big and dynamic. The chart also provides a quick view of the missing roles on the project and where the team could use extra staff. By looking at the organization chart, one can gauge the complexity of the project and the communication challenges. The tool is very helpful for the new joiners as they can understand the communication path and the hierarchy of the project very well just by looking at the org chart. The chart reduces the transition time for new project managers as it is clear to them who the key players in the project are and who they need to approach for what.

Typically, the PM is responsible for creating the project organization chart. Create the chart at the beginning of the project. It is easier to create when the project starts because you will have fewer people involved. Keep adding to the chart as the project expands. In the beginning, some roles might not have names; for example, the project may only have core members of the team assigned and it may not have identified the names of resources for the extended team that will come into the picture when the project reaches its peak. Names should be assigned against the roles as and when they become available, and the organization chart should be distributed as and when major changes to the project organization take place.

Work Breakdown Structure (WBS)

Someone has rightly said that "running a project without a WBS is like going to a strange land without a roadmap." The PMI defines a WBS as a deliverable-oriented hierarchical decomposition of the work to be executed by the project team to accomplish the project objectives and create the required deliverables. The purpose of the WBS is to ensure that the project includes and identifies all the work items needed to complete the project successfully without the addition of unnecessary work items. Therefore, the WBS organizes and defines the total scope of the project. As the name suggests, it breaks down or subdivides the project work into smaller and more manageable pieces of work, called work packages, with each descending level of the WBS representing an increasingly detailed definition of the project work. The planned work contained within the lowest-level WBS components, which are called work packages, can be scheduled, cost estimated, monitored, and controlled. From above explanations it is evident that WBS and project schedule are different. The work package is further decomposed into scheduling activities and scheduling tasks when the project schedule is being developed, so WBS is a step toward creating the project schedule. The WBS represents the work specified in the current approved project scope statement. Components comprising the WBS assist the stakeholders in viewing the deliverables of the project. The main advantage of the WBS is that it identifies all the work of the project in a structured and graphical way that is easy to read and understand. Apart from helping in scope management and schedule creation, the WBS also supports activity estimates both in terms of cost and time. One can roll up the lower-level deliverables or activities into higher parent-level deliverables, activities, or objectives.

Organizations generally maintain a standard WBS template that can be used for creating one for the project. The template can be modified to suit the needs of the project because every project is different. However, the basic structure would not change much from one project to another in the same organization. The WBS is supported by the WBS dictionary. The detailed content of the components contained in a WBS, including work packages and control accounts, can be described in the WBS dictionary. Each WBS component is cross-referenced, as appropriate, to other WBS components in the WBS dictionary. The WBS dictionary includes the description, cost, time, risk, resource, and scope of each activity or the work package.

As described, deliverables are decomposed to the work package level. The PM uses it to define the total scope of the project. The WBS should always be developed from the top down, and not the bottom up. Decomposition of the total project work generally involves the following activities:

- Identifying the deliverables and the related work
- Structuring and organizing the WBS
- Decomposing the upper WBS levels into lower-level, detailed components
- Developing and assigning the identification codes to the WBS components
- Verifying that the degree of decomposition of the work is necessary and sufficient

The WBS can be structured and organized into many forms – by project phase, by project components (subprojects), by functional area, by the type of work, etc. Work should be broken down based on the need of the team, convenience, and complexities.

Figure 3.22 is a simple example of the WBS for a project; however, it will be quite big and vast in real life. This concept can be extended to program management, where a program can have multiple projects, each project will have many phases, and each phase in turn will have deliverables, activities, and tasks. Similarly, if the project work is organized based on the functional area, then for a building construction project, the WBS can have Architecture, Civil, Electrical, Plumbing, and Landscaping at the second level. Each of these major functions can then be divided into mid-level work, lower mid-level work (if required), and the bottom level work (such as a task or activity).

Creating a WBS is a team effort; the PM is supposed to take the lead, while core team members and subject matter experts participate in the process and provide required inputs. WBS creation is a time-consuming effort and requires involvement from experts, stakeholders, customers, and various interest groups. One must be very patient and organized while doing this exercise. Similar to the project plan and project schedule, in the early stage of a project, it may be feasible to develop only a two- or three-level work breakdown structure because all the details of the project may not be available. As the project advances and more details become available, the WBS can be expanded and elaborated. Whenever there is a change in scope through a change control (change request) exercise, the WBS should also be changed to reflect the changed scope.

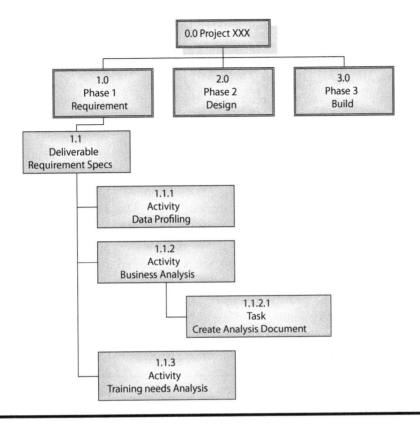

Figure 3.22   Simple example of the WBS for a project.

Decision Tree Diagram

As the name suggests, this is a diagram that looks like a tree and helps in making decisions in complex scenarios when multiple options are available. When there are many unknown routes available to reach a destination, each route is full of its share of humps and bumps, and the team is unsure about which path to take, a decision tree diagram helps solve the puzzle scientifically. The decision tree is also called a *tree diagram*. It is a decision support tool that uses a graph or model of decisions and their possible consequences, including chances of event outcomes, resource costs, and utility. A decision tree is used to identify the strategy most likely to reach a goal. This can be used as a predictive model for mapping from observations about an item to conclusions about its target value. In tree structures, leaves represent classifications and branches represent groups of features that lead to those classifications. So, the tool should be used for analysis of complex decisions where there are a number of factors contributing toward numerous outcomes and each outcome has uncertainties involved.

The decision tree is an effective decision-making tool for the following reasons:

- Clearly lays out the problem so that all options can be properly reviewed
- Allows full analysis of the possible consequences of a decision
- Provides a framework to quantify the values of outcomes and the probabilities of achieving them
- Helps make the best decisions on the basis of existing information and best guesses

Two examples of decision tree analysis are given in Figure 3.23 and Figure 3.24; it could be as simple as in Figure 3.23 or it could have complex quantitative analysis involved as shown in Figure 3.24.

The first exmaple is simple and straightforward. David is the manager of a famous golf club. Sadly, he is having some trouble with his customer attendance. There are days when everyone wants to play golf and the staff is overworked. On other days, for no apparent reason, no one plays golf and the staff has too much slack time. David's objective is to optimize staff availability by trying to predict when people will play golf. To accomplish that, he needs to understand the reason people decide to play and if there is any explanation for that. He assumes that weather must be an important underlying factor, so he decides to use the weather forecast for the upcoming week. So during two weeks he has been recording:

Independent Variables				Dependent Variable
Outlook	*Temperature*	*Humidity*	*Windy*	*Play*
Sunny	85	85	FALSE	Don't Play
Sunny	80	90	TRUE	Don't Play
Overcast	83	78	FALSE	Play
Rain	70	96	FALSE	Play
Rain	68	80	FALSE	Play
Rain	65	70	TRUE	Don't Play
Overcast	64	65	TRUE	Play
Sunny	72	95	FALSE	Don't Play
Sunny	69	70	FALSE	Play
Rain	75	80	FALSE	Play
Sunny	75	70	TRUE	Play
Overcast	72	90	TRUE	Play
Overcast	81	75	FALSE	Play
Rain	71	80	TRUE	Don't Play

Figure 3.23 Decision tree data.

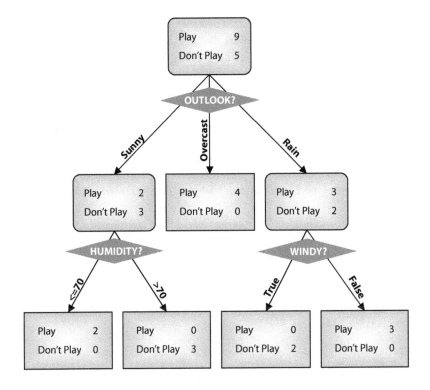

Figure 3.24   Decision tree.

- The outlook: whether it was sunny, overcast, or raining
- The temperature (in degrees Fahrenheit)
- The relative humidity in percent
- Whether it was windy
- Whether people attended the golf club on that day

David then compiled this data set into a table as shown in Figure 3.23. The top node represents all the data. The classification tree algorithm concludes that the best way to explain the dependent variable (i.e., play) is by using the variable "Outlook." Using the categories of the "Outlook" variable, three different groups were found:

1. One that plays golf when the weather is sunny
2. One that plays when the weather is cloudy
3. One that plays when it's raining

David's first conclusion: if the outlook is overcast, people always play golf, and there are some fanatics who play golf even in the rain. Then he divided the sunny group in two. He realized that people don't like to play golf if the humidity is higher than seventy percent.

Finally, he divided the rain category in two and found that people will also not play golf if it is windy.

And here is the short solution to the problem given by the classification tree: David dismisses most of the staff on days that are sunny and humid, or on rainy days that are windy, because almost no one is going to play golf on those days. On days when a lot of people will play golf, he hires extra staff. The conclusion is that the decision tree helped David turn a complex data representation into a much easier structure.

In the example in Figure 3.25, solving the decision tree provides expected monetary value (EMV) for each alternative. Alternative to the highest EMV is the most favorable option. In this case, upgrading the existing product seems to have a better EMV ($49.0 MN) and so it is preferred over Building a new product, which has an EMV of $41.5 MN. This example illustrates that sometimes the problem can be very complex and a decision tree diagram may need to be used along with some other tools (e.g., EMV).

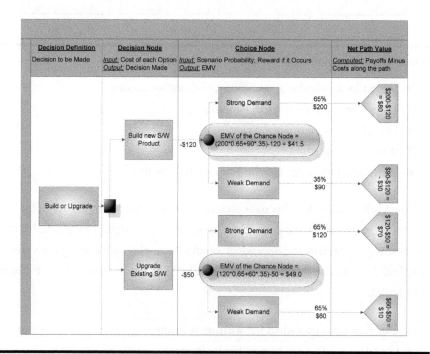

Figure 3.25   Decision tree.

Additional Project Schedule Reporting Tools

The Gantt chart and S curve were explained previously in this chapter. Apart from these two, there are some other simpler diagrams that can be used for illustrating project schedule; however, the occasion and purpose for which they can be used might be different. Look at Figure 3.26 and Figure 3.27, which can be plotted with the help of MS Visio. Figure 3.26 gives high-level timelines for the project in a simple view. Choose Timeline from the Project Schedule in MS Visio for plotting something similar to Figure 3.26. This diagram is very simple to draw and it is extremely easy to understand the high-level milestone schedule. Various descriptions and values can be added to the diagram to present suitable views to the team members and stakeholders. The powerful visual effect of this short diagram saves a lot of time for the stakeholders. Without digging into the gory details of the schedule, one can determine that the Design and Build phases of the project overlap for

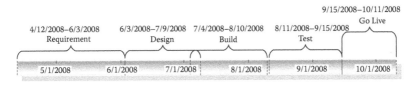

Figure 3.26 High level projection timeline.

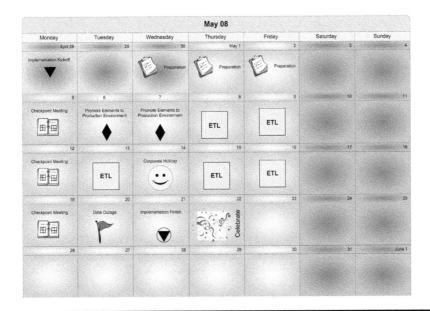

Figure 3.27 Schedule in calendar format.

about a week and there is a gap of one day between the end of the Build phase and the start of the Test phase. The diagram can be drawn in many shapes, such as a line, a block, or a cylinder. You can add milestone markers of different shapes and add short explanations to those milestones. There are convenient features that allow for changes to the time format and time scale. The percentage completion of the tasks/phases and the progress as of today's date can be shown quite easily on this diagram.

In the example in Figure 3.27, a particular group of tasks for the project (Implementation Tasks) are depicted in calendar format. Sometimes the project team likes to use such diagrams because they are easy to understand and maintain. So, depending on the circumstances and the need, different kinds of tools can be used to prepare and report schedule for the entire project or a part of it. This, however, does not eliminate the need for a comprehensive and detailed project schedule such as those created with the help of MS Project, Planview, or any other tool that your organization uses.

Chapter 4

Tables and Matrices

Oftentimes, project data needs to be systematically organized in order to analyze and compare a variety of characteristics. There is a famous proverb: "A clever person turns great problems into little ones." Tables and matrices help do exactly this as they show relationships between groupings that assist in structured problem solving. It is difficult to understand data in its abstract form. When it is grouped and placed side by side against other related groups, the relationship can be figured out and the project data can be analyzed and utilized better. Sometimes, a single data point or data set on its own does not make much sense, but when used in conjunction with other data, they prove quite useful. Projects produce, use, and store volumes of data that needs to be structured and organized in the form of tables and matrices for analysis, reporting, and other communication purposes. Data organization could be as simple as one-to-one mapping between the project roles and responsibilities, or as complex as a very huge project dashboard.

This chapter presents a variety of matrix-based tools. While some of them can be used as-is in the project plan, there are others that are quite useful for analysis and reporting purposes. These are a handful of standard tools, but there is no limit. Users can extend this basic knowledge for use in situations that are not identified in this book.

Responsibility Assignment Matrix (RAM)

The Responsibility Assignment Matrix (RAM) is used to illustrate the mapping between project task and human resource. That is, it connects the Work Breakdown Structure (WBS) to the Organization Breakdown Structure (OBS). For small projects, a single RAM captures the required information; but for large projects, RAMs

119

can be developed at multiple levels. A high-level RAM can define which department, unit, or team is responsible for each of the deliverables in the WBS. Lower-level RAMs are used within the group to assign roles, responsibilities, and levels of authorities for specific tasks. This allows team members to identify all activities associated with a person or to identify all the resources associated with one activity. The most common type of matrix is the RACI matrix (Figure 4.1). RACI is an acronym for Responsible Accountable Consult and Inform. The definition of each of these roles is given below; however, most of the time one will find organizations using only two types of roles: Owner and Approver. There can be several terms used for the purposes of a RAM. It is also known as a *linear responsibility chart* (LRC) and can be used to show who is responsible for what and at what level. For example, each row could represent a task and each column a person; the cells could then be assigned with the letters P (primary), S (secondary), and N (notify). This identifies the participants, and to which degree each activity will be performed and who will make decisions.

Figure 4.1 shows a simplistic example of RAM in RACI form. The WBS or the list of deliverables is placed in the left column as activities, and people or organization is shown along the horizontal line. One can use the role code (RACI or Owner/Approver) popular in one's organization for mapping the activity and responsible person. Not every resource will have an entry for each activity. The example in Figure 4.2 shows high-level tasks for a software development project, which can be broken down into lower-level tasks, and resource names can be assigned in place of generic names.

The RAM is a great communication tool that ensures that every project activity has roles and responsibilities assigned. Without a RAM, there often is confusion

Role	Definition
Responsible (R)	Owns the work and is responsible for performing the actual work. In case of a group work, R can be assigned to multiple people.
Accountable (A)	Confirms the completed work and is held fully accountable for it. There should be only one A.
Consulted ©	Person or group assigned to this role has the information and sometimes the capability to complete the work. Generally, the person responsible for the work consults the person performing this role. There is a two-way communication between R and C.
Informed (I)	Person or group assigned this role is to be informed of progress and results. Often there is a one-way communication from R to I.

Figure   RAM in RACI form.

Activities	Business User	Business Analyst	Developer	Tester	Project Manager
Requirement Definition	A				
Requirement Specifications	C	A	C	C	C
Design			A		
Build			A		
Test		C	R	A	
Implement	I	R	A	R	I

Figure 4.2   RAM as RACI.

about who owns the activity, who should be kept informed of the progress, who should be consulted, and who should review and approve the completed task. The matrix should be created in the beginning of the project before the detail work begins. Initially, every activity may not have resources assigned, so it is alright to leave the generic name against such activity instead of the actual resource name. The matrix should be prepared in consultation with the functional managers, resource managers, customer, and other stakeholders. Respective portions of the RAM, if the entire matrix is not appropriate, should be distributed to the project team, customer, and stakeholders, and signoff should be obtained. The table should be updated and distributed throughout the life of the project as and when it may be required.

One might wonder why a RAM is needed when a project has so many other communication tools that map activity and resource, either separately or in a combined way. Extra documentation and redundant processes should always be avoided. The project schedule captures resource information against every activity; the organization chart shows the areas/functions responsible for different project functions; and the roles and responsibility chart shows major project roles and their responsibilities. Then why do we need another document to capture similar information? A closer look reveals that none of the above tools provides information about the complete set of responsibilities and corresponding role/resource required for carrying out an activity. Every activity needs the involvement of various people in different capacities and their roles differ for that work. If the mapping of responsibility, role/resource, and activity is not documented properly, people will make assumptions about responsibilities, assumptions that may lead to confusion, friction, and delays later in the project. The RAM tool facilitates the preparation of project schedule, determination of resource requirements, and proper cost estimation. Project team members understand who they need to keep informed about the work activities so that they can get the right kind of feedback at the right time. If one understands who the right person is to approach for the right kind of information and right kind of job, then the job gets done faster. If more than one person is working on a task, it is imperative to designate one person who is accountable for the work; otherwise it will lead to confusion. Thus, the RAM plays an important role in project communication management.

Role and Responsibility Matrix

Roles and responsibilities must be identified for every project in order to complete the required tasks. This should address four items—role, authority, responsibility, and competency—to perform the role. This communication tool is part of the project human resource management area. The role and responsibility chart (see Figure 4.3) should be prepared in the beginning of the project while planning for human resources. Sometimes, this should be considered even before the scope definition exercise because what is required may also depend on who is available in the organization and in the marketplace to do it. All project roles should be defined up-front, and their responsibilities should be documented and distributed to the project team and other stakeholders. To make the tool complete, authority and competency should also be added. Most of the time, organizations have a standard role and responsibility chart that can be used in the project and, if needed, a slight modification can be done. Experts and resource managers should be involved in preparing the document. Resources are assigned roles based on their competencies. For example, a senior member of the technical team is sufficiently competent to take the role of lead designer. So, once the role is assigned to the person, he/she is also contacted about the responsibilities and authorities with respect to the project. When documented properly and communicated well, project team members and stakeholders have a clear understanding of who is responsible for what and who is authorized to make decisions on different matters. This avoids confusion and helps a great deal in communication.

Because this tool documents competencies against various roles, it facilitates resource assignment against all the roles. Resource managers understand the skill sets required for each role and staff the project accordingly. If competency is lacking, then training can be arranged for existing staff, a skilled resource can be hired from the marketplace, or the service of a vendor can be taken who can engage resources with the right competencies and skill sets. Thus, it also helps in identifying staff training needs and provides input into the hiring process. For example, the competency for a project manager (PM) might be documented as follows:

1. More than five years of project management experience in the relevant industry
2. Should have managed USD $2.0 million or larger project
3. Must be a PMI certified PMP

The tool should not only identify roles and responsibilities for project team members, but also for the project steering committee, project sponsor, senior management, vendor management lead, etc. The roles and responsibilities can be presented in text format or in table format (Figure 4.3). The examples show both presentation methods; but as one can see, the tabular format appears more effective in grabbing the reader's attention. When the resources are identified for each role, fill in the names to make the tool more useful.

Project manager: This is the person with authority to manage a project and who is responsible for the success of the project. This includes leading the planning and the development of all project deliverables. The PM is responsible for managing the budget, the schedule, and all project management procedures (scope management, issues management, risk management, etc.).

Designer: The designer is responsible for understanding the business requirements and designing a solution that will meet the business needs. There are many potential solutions that will meet the client's needs. The designer determines the best approach. A designer typically needs to understand how technology can be used to create this optimum solution for the client. The designer determines the overall model and framework for the solution, down to the level of designing screens, reports, programs, and other components. The designer also determines

Roles	Responsibilities

Figure 4.3   Roles and responsibility matrix (RAM).

the data needs. The work of the designer is then handed off to programmers and other people who will construct the solution based on the design specifications.

Communication Matrix

The communication matrix (see Figure 4.4) is part of the communication plan and is a very effective tool for establishing communication needs, channel, method, and frequency. This helps reduce confusion among the stakeholders regarding the communication process. The PM must ensure that team members, customers, users, and stakeholders have the information they need to perform their jobs. This helps manage expectations about the project communication needs and who needs to be doing what. This can be as simple as talking to team members about how they are doing on their assigned work, or holding a regularly scheduled status meeting. In whatever way it is done, proper communication is vital for project success. On smaller projects, communication is simple and may not require much proactive effort. However, communication becomes much more complex when the project gets bigger and more and more people get involved. Larger projects require communication to be planned in advance, taking into account the specific needs of the stakeholders involved. A communication matrix is useful in such situations because it facilitates efficient and effective communication with the various constituents. For effective communication, information should be provided in the right format, at the right time, to the right people. Efficient communication implies that only the required information is provided and nothing more.

The table in Figure 4.4 is short; however, in the real world, this table will be larger, involving all kinds of meeting and other communication needs with various stakeholders or groups of stakeholders. Make sure to identify all the required audiences up-front and make the matrix available to them in the planning phase of the project in order to set the course for the remaining project phases. Communication needs can change as the project moves forward, and thus the matrix can be changed to suit the changing needs of the project. If any of the stakeholders feel a need for change in the method or frequency of the communication, then the change can be discussed and implemented, if required. This tool ensures that all the important stakeholders have an opportunity to participate in the communication process appropriately, thus avoiding any chance of future conflict.

Project Team Roster

The project team roster is nothing but a project contact list. This includes information on all project team members, their role, location (with time zone), phone number, email, etc. This may be a simple document, but it goes a long way in facilitating communication in the project. The PM should prepare the document at

Audience	Message	Method/Channel	Timing/Frequency
Core Project Team	Details; Task-related; Project progress	Team meetings, task-related meetings; Individual meetings; Task/review-specific email	Regularly-scheduled team meetings (weekly); And as needed
Project Steering Committee	Policy-related issues; Project progress	Groundwork via email; consensus work via team meetings, Status Report document	Monthly; And as needed
Governing Board	Project overview (basic understanding, high-level timeline)	Board meeting	Monthly
Technical Review Board	Technical Design	Technical Review Board meeting; Document versioning tool; Email	At least once in the Project Life Cycle; And as needed
Customer/User Group	Impact Analysis; Status; Issues, Risks; Testing plans	User Meetings; Emails	Weekly; As needed
PMO	Project Status; Guidance and feedback; Risks and Issues	PMO status meeting; Status Report document; Email	Weekly and as needed
Maintenance and Operation	Handover details; Issues and Risks	Meeting; Email; Handover document	Weekly meeting one month before the project deployment; Daily meeting for one week after deployment
Supplier/Vendor	Inventory details; Issues	Meetings; Emails	Weekly till all the items are supplied; Monthly after all the items are supplied till project end date; As needed

Figure 4.4 Communication matrix.

the beginning of the project and should keep it up-to-date as more people join the team. Ensure that all members of the team have access to the roster; they know that such a document exists and where it exists. This can be distributed periodically and should be put on the project website. This is especially helpful on big projects where there are a lot of people involved at different locations. The PMs may have admin staff on big projects. Creation, update, and distribution of the contact information can be comfortably delegated to the project administrative staff. Based on the process of the organization, functional managers can also be asked to ensure that the information is up-to-date for their staff.

Many projects use email distribution lists, which can be maintained by project administrative staff. Multiple distribution lists can be created for different logical groups, such as Project_All (for all team members of the project), Business (for all business participants), QA (for all quality testers of the project), etc. The use of a distribution list saves a lot of time for the PM and other team members. Additionally, it also ensures that critical people are not left out of communications and that they get the information on time. At the same time, if the distribution list is not maintained properly, then the use of this tool might backfire. So, the PM should ensure that the list is updated immediately—as and when the resources join and leave the project.

Figure 4.5 shows a sample project team roster. Extra fields can be added based on project need.

Risk Probability–Impact Matrix

The risk probability–impact matrix, sometimes called just a *risk matrix*, is used to create a communication tool that prioritizes and categorizes project risks. The matrix is often used for communicating vital risk information to the project team members and customers. Risks need to be prioritized according to their potential implications toward meeting project objectives. Typically, a look-up table is created using the probability and impact, and the risks are rated according to the table. The matrix is pretty flexible in the sense that one can use different scales and criteria for different categories of risk. For example, all technical risks can have one matrix; human resource related risks can have another risk matrix, etc. The flexibility allows making suitable adjustments in the scale of probability and impact in order to do proper justice with all kinds of risks. Every category cannot be evaluated on the same scale. An organization may be ready to take more risk in one area; however, it may not tolerate much risk in another area.

Organizations may have a general definition of the probability level and impact level. These definitions should be reviewed by the project team and the customers during the risk management planning process and, if required, should be tailored to suit the project needs. On a simple chart, the probability and impact values can range from "low" to "medium" to "high." This can further be expanded to add

Name	Organization	Location/Address	Office #	Cell #	Home #	Role	Email	Comments

Figure   **Project team roster.**

		Impact		
		Low	Medium	High
Probability	High	Medium	High	Very High
	Medium	Low	Medium	High
	Low	Very Low	Low	Medium

Figure 4.6   Risk probability–impact matrix 1.

"very low" and "very high" values. Probability values can also have a range from "very unlikely" to "almost certain." The project team needs to decide which scale is suitable for the project and for the specific risk category. Alternatively, numerical values can be assigned for the probability and impact. A probability of 0.1 means very low probability, whereas the probability of 0.9 means almost certain probability. The impact scale represents the significance of impact for each project objective, if a risk occurs. A negative impact signifies threat and a positive impact signifies opportunity. Scale values can be linear (e.g., 0.1, 0.3, 0.5, 0.7, 0.9) or nonlinear (e.g., 0.05, 0.1, 0.4, 0.8). Nonlinear scales may represent the organization's desire to avoid high-impact threats or exploit high-impact opportunities, even if they have relatively low probabilities. Plenty of practice and skills are required in using the nonlinear scales. The team should understand the significance of numbers and their relationship to each other, how they were derived, and the effect they may have on different objectives of the project. A simple example is shown in Figure 4.6, where both the probability and impact have "Low," "Medium," and "High" values. Because the resultant of risk is the multiplication of probability and impact, the risks falling in the top right-hand corner can be categorized into the "Very High" zone and those falling into the lower left-hand corner can be categorized into the "Very Low" zone (Figure 4.6). Sometimes color codes are used in the matrix; for example, the three cells in the top right corner can be highlighted in red and, as a rule of thumb, the project team should focus on dealing with those risks first.

The risk matrix is used to determine the overall risk of the project. In the examples shown in Figure 4.6 and Figure 4.7, out of the total twenty identified risks, most of the risks fall in the "Very High" and "High" risk zones, while very few are in the "Medium," "Low," and "Very Low" zones. In looking at this matrix, the PM, customer, and senior management can quickly determine that this project is at very high risk. The risk prioritization exercise should be reviewed to determine that the matrix correctly represents all the risks. A cost–benefit analysis should be done to analyze what it will take to minimize and eliminate the "very high" risks. If the investment outweighs the returns, senior management may decide to terminate the project and resume once the risk factors decrease. The probability impact matrix

Impact				
Probability		Low	Medium	High
	High	18	19, 20	1, 3, 4, 5, 7, 10, 12, 13
	Medium			2, 6
	Low	15, 17	8, 9`	14, 16

Figure 4.7 Risk probability–impact matrix 2.

also indicates where the project team should focus their energies to gain maximum results. One should always look toward the top right-hand corner because that is the danger zone.

Risk Register

Risk management is a very tricky job; it requires a lot of skills and strategy. It is one of the most difficult tasks in project management. One of the basics of risk management is the creation and maintenance of Risk Register. The risk register helps track all risks within the project, so it is also called the risk log. Risk Register provides a key tool for risk management, as it holds all of the information relating to risks within the project. It is part of the project plan. Using the risk register, one can record the current status of each risk, and take the actions needed to reduce or enhance the likelihood of it occurring. The tool helps in performing a risk response planning exercise that results in the documentation of potential responses in the register. Plans are made and actions are taken to reduce the probability and impact of the harmful risk and enhance those of the positive risk.

The risk register is a great communication tool because it helps in making everyone, including senior management and the customer, aware of the potential risks on the project, strategy of the project team to deal with those risks, where the team needs attention from senior management, etc. It serves as a great escalation tool that provides the PM with an opportunity to garner adequate senior management support for the project. It works as a tool to warn the project team, steering committee, customer, senior management, and other stakeholders about the impending danger so that appropriate steps can be taken on time to safeguard project interests. The manner of risk documentation and escalation goes a long way in the success and/or failure of a project. Just the creation and distribution of a risk register is not enough, however; the PM should proactively work toward the implementation of the risk response actions according to the risk management plan. The risk register should be reviewed and updated, if required, at least every week. Update may be needed for many things; there may be new risks identified, priorities of the risks may change based on many factors, there can be changes to the risk response, the dates may need to be updated, the probability might change. It is a good practice to attach the risk register to the weekly project status report.

Risk management can be made easy and very effective if the risk register is created at the right time with the participation of core team members and subject matter experts, and is maintained throughout the project life cycle. The register is shared with the team as well as management and customers. The PM should take the lead in creating, maintaining, and distributing the risk register. The first step is to identify the potential risks to the project. Next, the team should list all possible responses to all the risks. Previously executed similar projects can provide a very good starting point. The project team can look into the risks that have occurred in those projects to find out at which stage they occurred and what strategies were adopted by the project team. Another very good pointer is the lessons learned document of old projects. Many problems can be avoided and minimized by referencing the risk registers and lessons learned documents of old projects. A wise person learns from others' mistakes.

The table in Figure 4.8 provides information that is typically captured in a risk register. An explanation of the terms is provided in parentheses against each term for better understanding. On smaller projects, risks may not need to be categorized; however, for large and complex projects, there can be so many risks that they are required to be categorized for better tracking and handling. The *risk breakdown structure* (RBS) categorizes risks into a hierarchical tree-like structure. So, on very complex projects, there can be major categories, which in turn can have several subcategories. Examples of major categories include technical, cost, schedule, external, project management, etc. Subcategories for external risk can include raw material, market, customer, vendor, government, etc. The RBS is updated from time to time whenever new risks are identified. The root cause of the risk is identified through brainstorming, the fishbone diagram technique, etc. The team decides on the probability, impact, and priority of every risk. The probability–impact matrix, described as a separate topic in this chapter explains in detail how the probability and impact values are assigned to the risks, and how the risk score is obtained using the probability and impact values. It is very important to identify the owner of the risk. There must be just one owner for any risk; it might be the PM, the customer, the vendor, the senior executive, a team lead, etc. More than one owner causes confusion. Sometimes more than one risk can have same risk score; in that case, the value in the priority column decides the order in which the risks should be taken care of. Risk response is explained in great detail in the book in the "risk management plan" section. Apart from the fields mentioned in the table below, sometimes people use risk symptoms, cost and budget information, project parameters that may be impacted, etc.

The PM can decide to use two different registers: one for the low score risks and one for high score risks. The low score risk register can be used just as a watch-list

Risk #	Risk Description (List of identified risks)	Risk Category (If the Organization maintains Risk Category and if project maintains RBS, then it is needed; otherwise ignore)	Root Cause of Risk	Probability	Impact	Risk Score (product of Probability and Impact; can also be obtained through a Probability Impact Matrix Look-up table)	Owner	Priority	List of Potential Responses	Date When Risk Occurred	Response Taken	Date When Response Taken

Figure 4.8 Risk register.

so that it is monitored less frequently, while the high score risk register can be used to review and update on a regular basis.

Requirements Traceability Matrix (RTM)

A requirements traceability matrix (RTM) is invariably used in software development projects; however, it's difficult to imagine why this wonderful tool cannot be utilized in other industries. To define it in a simple way, let us look at the three words that make this term. *Requirement* is another name for the business need or condition to meet a new or altered product. *Traceability* refers to the completeness of the information about every step in a process chain. *Matrix* (plural matrices) is a rectangular table of elements or entries. So, RTM is nothing but a tabular representation of various distinct requirements (explicit or derived) and important deliverables in different stages of the SDLC (software development life cycle). It establishes a relationship for every deliverable to its predecessor and successor (unless it is the final product). This relationship also determines dependencies among the various project elements. Every distinct requirement is given a requirement ID (RI). These RIs are shown as rows of the MS Excel spreadsheet and major deliverables form the columns of the spreadsheet. The matrix links High-Level Requirement to Detailed Requirement to High-Level Design to Detailed Design to Code Element to Test Case. It can be easily understood from the example shown in Figure 4.9.

Software is developed in stages or phases, where the work product of each stage can be associated with the work products of the previous stage. This provides the ability to trace the requirements through the work products (*forward traceability*) and from the work products back to the requirements (*backward traceability*). Depending on the organization's standards and development practices, the work products of intermediate stages might vary.

RTM is primarily used for quality control so that it can be ensured that customer requirements are met. It also helps the developer find out why some code was developed in certain ways, by being able to go from the code to the requirements. If a test fails, it is possible to use the RTM to see what requirements or code the test relates to. It is very common to find out at a later stage in the project that some requirement is completely missed. This proves very costly to the project. With the help of RTM, such costly mistakes can be avoided. There are some mission-critical projects, where one cannot afford to miss even a single, small requirement. A simple miss in a space mission might cause a huge disaster. Similarly, on a security and regulatory project, one small lapse can cause a tremendous amount of damage to the organization. Sometimes, the RTM is mandated by the customer. The RTM achieves the following goals:

Requirement ID	High-Level Requirement	Analysis Stage			Design Stage	Build Stage	Testing Stage	
		Project Charter Reference	Detailed Requirement	Requirements Document Reference	Functional Specs Reference	Module/Interface Reference	Test Plan Reference	Test Script Reference
P1111A-1	Enable the development of standard reporting to support and grow the Full-tab program.	P1111A_Project Definition_v1.3 Section 3.1/ Page 6	Need to add an indicator to Claims table.	P1111A_Business_Requirement_Document v1.1 Section 3.1/Page 15	P1111A_Functional Specs v1.0 Sections 2.2 and 2.4 Page # 5, 6	Name of Program/Module and a reference to the section/paragraph of the code	P1111A_Test Plan v1.0 Section 3.1/ Page 5	P1111A_Test Script v1.0 Test Case # 1-4 and 6-7
P1111A-2	Enable the development of standard reporting to support and grow the Full-tab program.	P1111A_Project Definition_v1.3 Section 3.1/ Page 6	ETL code will need to be changed to pick up the new field Tablet Splitting Indicator (1 byte).	P1111A_Business_Requirement_Document v1.1 Section 3.1/Page 16	P1111A_Functional Specs v1.0 Sections 2.3 and 2.5 Page # 5, 7	Name of Program/Module and a reference to the section/paragraph of the code	P1111A_Test Plan v1.0 Section 3.2/ Page 5	P1111A_Test Script v1.0 Test Case # 5 and 8-10
P1111A-3	Enable the development of standard reporting to support and grow the Full-tab program.	P1111A_Project Definition_v1.3 Section 3.1/ Page 6	The new field should have specific valid values ('U','Y','N').	P1111A_Business_Requirement_Document v1.1 Section 3.1/Page 16	P1111A_Functional Specs v1.0 Sections 2.3 and 2.5 Page # 5, 7	Name of Program/Module and a reference to the section/paragraph of the code	P1111A_Test Plan v1.0 Section 3.2/ Page 5	P1111A_Test Script v1.0 Test Case # 5 and 8-10
P1111A-4	Make 3 years historical values of HTI available in Database	P1111A_Project Definition_v1.3 Section 3.1/ Page 6	Back-load Rx Claim table for 3 years of data to update HTI field from the source.	P1111A_Business_Requirement_Document v1.1 Section 3.1/Page 17	P1111A_Functional Specs v1.0 Sections 2.6 Page # 9	Name of Program/Module and a reference to the section/paragraph of the code	P1111A_Test Plan v1.0 Section 3.3/ Page 7	P1111A_Test Script v1.0 Test Case # 11-15

Figure 4.9　Requirements traceability matrix.

1. Ensures that the approved requirements are addressed in all phases of SDLC from Planning & Analysis to Design to Development to Testing to Deployment.
2. Ensures that each deliverable is traceable. Test Cases should be traceable to requirements; modules and code should be traceable to business and functional specifications. This will ensure that no extra work is performed in the project and all the deliverables are made to satisfy one requirement or another.
3. Analyze the impact of a change. Because the RTM establishes a relationship among various project elements, it illustrates how a change in one element will impact other elements or deliverables of the project.

Follow the steps below to create an RTM:

1. Collect high-level requirements from the project charter, proposal document, or project scope document — Business Analyst (BA).
2. Detail the requirements in the business requirements document — BA.
3. Start filling out the RTM template with each distinct requirement — BA.
4. Ensure that every requirement has a unique Requirement ID — BA.
5. The RTM in this state should be reviewed by the Business Analysis review team as well as the project team so as to verify that nothing has been missed — PM/BA.
6. Get signoff on the RTM from client when they sign off on the business requirements document — PM.
7. Every time a requirement changes, it should reflect into the RTM — BA.
8. Once the requirements document is complete, developers/designers and testers take this up and fill out details of section/page # from Design document (developer/designer) and Test Case #/Test Case document name (Tester) in order to map each and every requirement correspondingly.
9. The RTM in this form should be reviewed whenever the team reviews the design document and test case document.
10. Once coding is complete, each code element/program name/module name should be entered against the requirement to which they correspond.

The example in Figure 4.9 illustrates how the tool should be created and updated. Note that for the purposes of this example, there are two main objectives or high-level requirements (HLRs). These HLRs regenerate into multiple detail requirements. Each of these detail requirements should be identifiable through a unique Requirement ID. The HLRs, which "enable the development of standard reporting to support and grow the full-tab program," have three detail requirements, so there are three unique IDs for them. Each of these unique requirements (IDs) should be tracked through Planning, Design, Build, Test, and Implementation phases. There may be fewer unique requirements at the beginning of the project—up until requirements are not detailed out—but the number grows as requirements are fleshed out to minor details.

If the requirements are tracked this way, it can be ensured that BA has not missed detailing every objective, the designer/developer has coded for all the detail requirements, and the tester has tested each of them. If a test case fails, it is very easy to track which requirement and objective it is mapped to, so the team can know which particular objective is not yet met.

There are some industry-standard tools available to perform the RTM, such as Rational RequisitePro. In cases when no such tool is available, one can be created using MS Excel. The example shown in Figure 4.9 is a very simple RTM but in real life it can be lengthy and very huge. This is a time-consuming exercise and employees generally find it as overhead and boring; however, if practiced on time and done properly, this can save a lot of rework and enhance product quality tremendously. The PM and QA lead should take special interest in this process to drive the entire team. The business analyst (BA) can also champion this process. Sometimes, people make this process complicated and finally give up midway after expending enormous effort, which discourages the team and the organization from taking this up again in subsequent projects. So, try to keep this as simple as possible in order to seek participation from every team member and thereby to complete the process easily and effectively.

Quality Matrix

The quality matrix is part of the quality plan and should be developed early in the project in consultation with the customer and the quality lead. As the name suggests, it is a table that lists the required project performance level for identified quality parameters. This is a reflection of the expectation levels of the customer and is often referred to as the *acceptance criteria* for the project. If all the details are not available at the beginning of the project, then make sure that they are available at least before the testing or the quality check starts. In such a case, the lack of a quality matrix can be a huge risk for the project, so this risk should be documented and communicated to the customer and the senior management on a regular basis. High quality expectations might lead to rigorous and multiple rounds of testing that, in turn, can raise the project cost. Similarly, if the number of quality parameters is greater, then testing scope and coverage will need to be expanded, thus leading to increased project cost. That is, there is a delicate balance between the quality expectations and the project cost. It is the job of the PM to carefully evaluate these two factors and report extra requirements of budget in order to meet the accepted quality matrix. For example, suppose you are a PM working for a coal mining company. The company signs a contract with a new steel manufacturer that requires a very high grade of coal for its blast furnace. With the current setup of the beneficiation plant, your company can only provide coal with 17 percent or more ash. The new customer needs coal with less than 14 percent ash and more than 13.0 percent ash in the raw material. This requires your company to enhance the current coal beneficiation facility to meet the demands of this customer. The cost of the project is estimated at $1.5 million to meet the quality demand. However, a couple of months into the planning phase, the customer has raised the quality bar and now demands that all coal supplies should contain ash content in the range between 13.0 percent and 13.7 percent. This will clearly require more budget for the project because you will need to purchase and install an extra set of screening equipment in the mineral beneficiation plant. Similarly, on a software development project, the demand from the customer to supply the product with two "severity 5" defects will lead to higher total project cost than, say, the requirement of three defects of "severity 5 per 1000 hours of work."

Once the quality parameters and corresponding performance levels are identified and agreed upon, pass this on to all functional areas/units/organizations of the project. All functional areas need to build a corresponding matrix for their deliverables so that quality is not just validated, verified, and tested at the end, but rather that they are assured and controlled at every step of the process according to the individual quality goals that are aligned with the final quality goal and quality matrix of the project. This is *Total Quality Management (TQM)*. Take an example of a software development project with an estimated effort of 2000 hours. The customer lays out the quality goals for scope (in terms of number of severity 1 defects), schedule, and cost as shown in the matrix in Figure 4.10.

How can the quality goals can be set and met in the project? As per the above quality requirement, for a 2000-hour project, the maximum number of acceptable "severity 1" defects in the final product would be four. So, as a PM, you need to set quality goals for all the major processes in consultation with the functional leads and the quality lead. The inputs that go into this planning are the historical data from similar projects executed by the organization in the past, human resource consideration (skill and training), and schedule and cost considerations. The study of past projects provides data for the defect injection rate and defect detection rate. Once all the inputs are factored into this data, the defect injection and defect detection rates can be set for every process/deliverable in the project. Once the rate for the project is set as above, the next step is to calculate and set the goal for the absolute

Parameter	Quality Goal
Severity 1 Defect in final product	2 defects per 1000 hrs
Schedule Variance	30 days
Cost Variance	10%

Figure 4.10   Quality matrix 1.

defect numbers at every stage/process. The goal for the absolute number of defects injected/detected at each stage can be calculated by multiplying the corresponding rates with the total number of hours allocated to each stage/process. Suppose for this project that the BA can afford to inject ten defects in the requirements analysis, out of which the review process of the requirements document should detect nine of those. One of the defects can go unnoticed or undetected and is passed on to the next stage. Similarly, suppose that by multiplying the rate with the corresponding design effort, the designer can afford to inject twenty defects and the design review process should catch sixteen of them, including or excluding the one requirement defect passed on from the previous phase. While extending the calculation this way, at the end of the project the total number of defects injected and detected should be sixty and fifty-six, respectively. The difference of four defects remains in the product, which complies with the quality goal set by the customer. Apart from planning this matrix, there must be another plan to ensure that these goals are met. This is good for planning, but you will always find that while monitoring and comparing the actual status with the planned matrix as shown in Figure 4.11, there will be a lot of variance in both the defect injection and defect detection numbers. If the difference is too large, there must be something wrong either in the planning or in the execution of the plan. Notwithstanding the variance, this will provide the PM, senior management, and other leads an opportunity to evaluate and analyze the quality status at each and every major milestone and take corrective action if required. Goals can be set for future processes upon the availability of more details and insight. Suppose that only ten defects were discovered in the code review process against the goal of twenty-two defects. What does this imply? Either the coding was very good so that significantly fewer defects were injected, or the review process was faulty so it could not find the defects. Most of the time, one can take a guess on what might be the major reason. If the programmers were very experienced and strong, then we can accept this result. On the contrary, if (a)

Process	Defect Injected	Defect Detected
Requirement	10	9
Design	20	16
Construction	30	22
Testing	0	8
Post Deployment	0	1
Total	60	56

Figure 4.11   Process defect matrix.

the reviewers were not well versed in the system, process, or the code, or (b) enough time was not spent on review, then we can confidently assume that there was a gap in the review and so there is a greater chance that more defects might pass on to the testing phase. As a corrective action, either the code could be recommended for group review or a decision could be made to do more rigorous testing. Both of these have their own merits and demerits. Group review is a costly affair, so it should be practiced judiciously.

In another situation, suppose that the reviewers found thirty defects during code review; what does that imply? If the review process is very good, then one can be confident that the reviewers have done a good job and have identified all or most of the defects injected so far, including those in the previous stages. Looking at it from another angle, if you think the reviewers are not extraordinary and their performance is representative of the organization's historical statistical data of defect detection rate, then you can expect that more defects were injected in the coding, hence more than eight defects should be detected in the testing phase too. So, there is no single answer for these results, and one should carefully evaluate and analyze the data, keeping in mind all the environmental and other factors.

In similar fashion, internal targets can be set for schedule and budget for each and every process. Some projects keep buffers in terms of internal goals. This depends on the confidence of senior management on the project team, the complexity of work, the criticality of the project, the tolerance level of the customer, etc. The status should be reported to and discussed regularly with senior management. As described above, if quality matrix is planned and tracked properly, then it helps meet customer expectations in a managed and controlled fashion and prevents customer dissatisfaction, sanctions, and penalties.

Issue Log

The issue log is one of the important project communication tools. Issues are part and parcel of every project. They should be handled properly because unresolved issues can be a major source of conflict and project delay. An issue log is the tool that can be used to document and monitor the resolution of issues. Sometimes it is also called *issue list* or *action item log*. Issues are addressed in order to maintain good constructive working relationships among the various stakeholders, including team members.

The difference between risk and issue was discussed earlier in this book under "Risk Management Plan" (see Chapter 2). They not only differ by definition but also in the way they are managed in the project. The manner in which project issues are managed is documented in the "Issue Management Plan" section of the project management plan. The issue management plan describes the process to manage and control project issues. It documents the process to identify project issues and a systematic way to handle the issues until they are resolved. The plan explains steps

Issue #	Issue Name	Description	Status (Open, Closed, Deferred)	Raised by	Assigned to	Date Reported	Expected Resolution Date (ETA)	Final Resolution	Remarks
1									
2									
3									

Figure 4.12 Issue list.

to control issues and minimize their impact on project parameters. It serves as a guide for the project team, senior management, customer, and other stakeholders to identify, control, and manage the issues. The plan covers information on the tools and techniques for reporting an issue, tracking mechanism, escalation procedure, reporting methods, roles and responsibilities, and the steps to close the resolved issues. The lack of an issue management process leads to utter chaos in the project, low employee morale, high friction, and ultimately the failure of the project in meeting its objectives. Issues can arise from Day One of the project, but the project plan cannot be ready on Day One. So, although the PMs will not have a documented elaborate issue management process in place on Day One, they should at least start using the issue log. Later, the process should briefly be explained and mentioned during the project kickoff meeting where all the stakeholders and team members are present. That will make everybody understand that the project has an issue management practice in place and will also make them aware of their roles and responsibilities, along with a high-level understanding of the process. Later, when an elaborate project plan is prepared, which has the issue management plan either embedded or referenced separately, it can be communicated and discussed with the team. Among other tools, the issue management plan provides information on the issue tracking tool.

An issue should be documented in such a way that it helps in resolving it. An owner is generally assigned and a target date is established for closure. Most organizations have standard tools, such as Mercury Quality Center, Rational Clear Quest, or any other in-house tool, to track issues as well as defects. In case there is no standard tool or for some reason you end up not using the tool, then use an MS Excel spreadsheet-based issue list. This is a very effective communication tool if prepared and updated properly and in a timely fashion. Issues should be reviewed and updated at least on a weekly basis. Use the fields as shown in the example in Figure 4.12. If the list is very long, it can be managed better by adding a few more fields, such as Category, Responsible Unit/Area, Criticality, Priority, etc. If you want to collect enough data to analyze the cause of issues for the purpose of prevention in future projects, it can be tracked in a manner the organization usually employs to tracks defects. Add some fields—such as Root cause, Stage when injected, Stage when detected, Artifact/Deliverable having the issue, etc.

Sometimes, on big projects, there can be several issues at any one point in time, and it may not be possible to work on all the issues simultaneously. This situation necessitates that the issues be ranked and ordered in priority for the project team to understand the order in which they need to address the issues. The issue prioritization process should be explained in the issue management plan. Issues are compared against each other on various factors, such as impact to project parameters (schedule, cost, quality, safety, etc.); effort required to resolve the issue; dependency of other identified issues on the issue being considered; etc. Often, input is collected from subject matter experts, customers, and project team members. Ranking can be made more scientific by assigning values to the project factor getting impacted and the impact severity, and then computing the value of "ranking level" by multiplying the two. The issue with the highest ranking level is given higher priority. So, if Issue #1 has a ranking level of 8 and Issue #2 has a ranking level of 12, then Issue #2 will be given higher priority than the Issue #1. Issue ranking level computation can be a very time-consuming and tedious process, requiring tremendous amounts of time from the PM and other participants.

Issue ranking level = Impact severity × Value of the project factor

Suppose that, for a mining project, safety is the number-one constraint, followed by cost, followed by schedule. Then one can assign values 4, 3, and 2, respectively, to safety, cost, and schedule. So, if a particular issue has a very high impact (severity level 5) on safety, a medium impact (severity level 3) on cost, and very low impact (severity level 1) on schedule, then the ranking level of the issue can be computed as follows:

Ranking level = (5 × 4) × (3 × 3) × (1 × 2) = 20 × 9 × 2 = 360

Here, the project factors have been assigned values of 4, 3, and 2. This assignment depends on the tolerance of the customer related to various project factors and the organization's process for assigning values.

Issues arise throughout the life of the project and thus a list is helpful at every stage. On a very small project, a single issue list created at the beginning of the project can be carried out and maintained through to the end of the project. However, on large projects, multiple issue lists can be created based on the relevant business areas, stage of the project, technical domain, etc. They can be maintained until the relevant work continues, and can be closed and archived once that work finishes. Any open issue can then be transferred to the newer issue list. The creation of multiple lists is convenient for usage and maintenance. When the project starts, one would like to have requirements analysis, planning, and architectural discussions within the project. This might be twice a week or a daily activity where the core project team meets and discusses various items and brainstorms on critical topics. Several questions can be raised, which may require further analysis and investigation. The *expected turnaround* (ETA) can be determined and action items can be assigned to various team members, including the PM, and then they can be tracked through the issue list. The team can discuss the open items, the status of action items and any new topics in the next meeting, and the issue list is updated in the meeting. So, at the initial stages, the issue list can work as an agenda item for the team meetings and guide the project team through the planning meetings, requirements analysis discussion meetings, and architectural discussion meetings.

Project managers play a very important role in managing project issues. They should never delegate this task to anyone else in the project. It is critical that PMs understand issues at least on a high level and track every issue themselves.

Other team members can add issues, change status, or even close them, but they must notify the PM before making any change to the list. Project managers must understand and be convinced of the status change and the resolution entered against the project. As far as possible, PMs should update the issue log themselves. This practice ensures that they stay on top of the issues and understand the implications of the issues so that corrective action can be planned and initiated on time. Project managers who do not pay enough attention to proper issue management are doomed to fail. You might have seen team members discussing issues referring to emails, or some conversation, or some meeting. They will first take time to remind everyone of the existing issue and then discuss the status and next steps without ever documenting the issues properly. This is fatal, as without proper tracking it is difficult to stay on top of all the issues and to bring them to timely closure. This may also lead to issues falling through the cracks despite all efforts by the project team. So, the PM should act very seriously on the issue management front. The issue management process should be communicated to the team members and the stakeholders in the beginning of the project and afterwards the PM should take the lead in documenting and tracking all project issues.

Issue reporting is generally part of weekly project status reporting. Report the total number of open issues, along with a list of all critical issues. Issues are one of the main inputs for the project status report to senior management and the customer. This can also go along with the project milestone report as well as phase gate/exit gate/toll gate report. Apart from this, the PM should bring up the critical issues in the project steering committee meeting, clearly stating the current status, what is being done to resolve the issues, and what situation prevents the issues from being closed on time. One should never hide issues from senior management. If reported honestly and in a timely manner, the PM would not only get suggestions from experienced members of senior management, but would also get support in terms of capital, resource, logistics, etc.

Project Dashboard

The dashboard used in cars and other motor vehicles provides vital information on key parameters to the driver. Based on indicators in the dashboard, drivers make appropriate decisions, such as refueling the vehicle, taking it to the garage, resting the vehicle, etc. Similarly, a project dashboard provides vital information to the PM and upper management on key project parameters so that they can recognize the problem on time and can take appropriate action. With a quick glance at the dashboard, one can understand the health of the project and can catch symptoms of potential problems. The project schedule may be on track, but resources may be working overtime to meet the deadline; and at this burn rate, the cost may eventually go way beyond the budget. In another project, the schedule and budget may be on track, but the defect detection rate may be low during the initial few phases, indicating potential major defects toward the end or after the project goes live. The late discovery of defects may derail the schedule and cost equations. So, when data for all these vital parameters is available side by side, it becomes easy to obtain a holistic view of project health and impending issues. Executives rarely have time to read through the detailed status reports covering all aspects of the project. The project dashboard gives them the needed information in the most effective and concise way.

Just as the dashboard in a car provides running and dynamic information to the driver at every moment, the project dashboard provides up-to-date, live information about the project. If the information is stale, it is of no use. So, the PM, PMO, and project administrative team must create the tool in such a way that it can provide live and up-to-date information to senior management. Ideally, the tool should be automated to take detailed information from different project databases and present a dashboard view for a project or group of projects. Whatever the method, automatic or manual, the dashboard should be kept up-to-date; otherwise, it will not provide immediate information. Another important aspect of the dashboard is that it should be catering to the needs of senior management and the customer; otherwise, the entire effort may go to waste and may not serve the purpose for which it is being built. So, the PM should solicit regular feedback on the content and format. This helps management save time by preventing the need to go through multiple reports for critical project information. The dashboard is most helpful during execution as well as the monitoring and controlling processes.

There are a variety of project management tools and applications available in the marketplace, and organizations use one tool or another. If your organization does not have one, a dashboard can be created in MS Excel. Sometimes, project team members or team leads can fill in data for their respective tasks/deliverables and then detailed data can be summarized through programming, macros, or script to provide information on the project health parameters. Standard project management tools have these macros built into the tool. Dashboards in every such tool have a different look and feel; most of the time they can be customized. In general, it should provide a status on schedule, budget, resource, open high priority, and critical defects/issues (age of open defects and their number), EVA, etc. Dashboard creation is not a one-time effort; it is dynamic in nature. Make sure that the structure and format are maintainable and scalable. The format may need to be changed from time to time, depending on the needs of senior management.

The dashboard is generally used for program and portfolio management. It is very helpful in enterprise project management, where you can prepare dashboard reports for all the projects and can compare them on different vital parameters for decision making. Data from multiple projects can be rolled up into a consolidated view to generate vital information for the program and portfolio. The dashboard should be made available at a centralized location where everyone can access it whenever required. Program managers manage multiple related projects and it always helps to prepare a grid for all the projects and track important information that they might need most frequently. Some projects involve enhancements or developments to multiple business applications and business areas. In this case too, tracking important metrics information helps. Project managers need to provide information on different parameters to the executives and sometimes the information is needed immediately. Most of the time, this information will be available in emails. Even if the project emails are organized properly, it might take time to search for all the data. Once the data is available, then it might take time to organize and structure it the way upper management wants it. The project dashboard, often referred to as *project metrics*, helps avoid such last-minute scampering. If the dashboard is placed at a central location and is updated regularly, then senior management need not reach out to the PMs. This saves a lot of valuable time and energy for the PM, the project team, and senior management. As you know, one phone call or one email from senior management can disturb the PM's entire schedule for the day, and nobody would like to be in that situation.

The example in Figure 4.13, which is created in MS Excel or some similar tool, will prove very handy. One can capture information relevant and important to a particular situation. Other variations might include information on the critical defect data (total number, number of defects open, number of defects older than a month, etc.); critical risks and issues; percentage of work completed; Earned Value Analysis (EVA); etc. Figure 4.13 can be supplemented with some relevant and useful charts and graphs, such as a column chart for cost data, a bar chart for resource data, a pie chart for defect distribution, an S curve, a line chart, etc. The format and content will differ significantly based on the project, program, portfolio, and senior management's needs. However, one should not add all the details to the dashboard. Information is always reported at a summary level, which is a strength as well as a limitation of the project dashboard. In general, the project dashboard should fit on one page and contain ten to fifteen fields. Visualize this in terms of the dashboard in an automobile. If the dashboard has too much detail, one may be overwhelmed by the extra details and miss the vital information that one requires instantaneously. It will become very difficult to maintain the dashboard that has too much detailed information.

Pivot Table

There are many good features available in spreadsheet applications such as MS Excel, of which special mention of the pivot table is made here because this is a very useful tool for PMs. The idea is not to describe each and every option of the pivot table or to explain how to create a pivot table; rather, it is to make one aware of this excellent feature that one will be happy to implement once one knows how and when to use it. When large amounts of data are available in raw format and one wants to pick and choose data fields and then present them in different views, this

Proj #	Project Name	Proj Type	Customer/ Sponsor	Planned Start Date	Actual Start Date	Planned Finish Date	Actual Finish Date	Budget	Actual cost as of Date	Overall Status	Remarks

Figure 4.13 Project dashboard.

tool can be very helpful. Data can be grouped together by different classifications and then multiple aggregate actions can be performed—such as Sum, Sort, Average, Count, Min, Max, Standard Deviation, etc. Figure 4.14 illustrates one example of the raw data present in the Excel spreadsheet and a simple view created through a pivot table (Figure 4.15) for resource allocation per month by "Proj Manager" and by "Proj Number." In MS Excel, one selects the data that one wants to use for the pivot table, and then goes to the "Data" menu and selects the "PivotTable and PivotChart Report" option. The pivot table and chart can be created by dragging and dropping the fields that one wants to use.

In Figure 4.15, Role, Proj Type, and Status have not been used from the raw data. "Hrs allocated" and "Month" have been dragged up to the highest level from the "PivotTable Field List." Other fields—"Resource Name," "Project Mgr," and "Project Number"—are on a lower level.

In Figure 4.16, the effort data of resources for a particular week are downloaded from the effort tracking tool of the project. The raw data can have many more fields than are shown in the figure. But while creating the pivot table, one can choose to pick only a few fields that one requires for a report or for analysis.

Figure 4.17 provides information on the total hours worked by resources on two different projects for different deliverables and activities. See how the fields "Hours" and "Project" have been dragged all the way to the top and the fields "User," "Activity," and "Deliverable" are at lower levels. Try this example in MS Excel to get the hang of it.

The above data can be plotted to provide different views by dragging and dropping various fields very conveniently on the chart. Highlight the pivot table in Figure 4.17 by taking the cursor on the left of the left-most field of the table "Sum of Hours" and clicking on the field. Next, right-click on the highlighted area and select the "PivotChart" option. In this example, only "User" and "Activity" are chosen to plot against total hours for the projects. One can add or remove fields by right-clicking on the "User" and "Activity" boxes. Similarly, the chart can be modified by right-clicking different pieces of the chart. It is very easy to determine from the particular chart in Figure 4.18 that only three resources worked on Proj 1 in the week and all resources worked on Proj 2.

Resource Name	Role	Project Mgr	Project Number	Proj Type	Proj Status	Month	Hrs allocated
Sunny	Developer	Shankar	A1111	L	Open	Jan	20
Sunny	Developer	Shankar	A1111	L	Open	Feb	160
Sunny	Developer	Shankar	A1111	L	Open	Mar	150
Sunny	Developer	Shankar	A1111	L	Open	Apr	140
Sunny	Developer	Shankar	A1111	L	Open	May	120
Sunny	Developer	Jha	B2222	L	Open	May	40
Mona	BA	Jha	B2222	S	Open	Jan	120
Mona	BA	Jha	B2222	S	Open	Feb	100
Mona	BA	Jha	B2222	S	Open	Mar	90
Mona	BA	Jha	B2222	S	Open	Apr	160
Mona	BA	Jha	B2222	L	Open	May	40
Mona	BA	Shankar	A1111	L	Open	May	120
Pam	QA	Shankar	A1111	L	Open	Jan	90
Pam	QA	Shankar	A1111	L	Open	Apr	40
Donna	DBA	Jha	B2222	L	Open	May	5
Donna	DBA	Jha	B2222	S	Open	Jan	20
Donna	DBA	Jha	B2222	S	Open	Feb	40
Donna	DBA	Jha	B2222	S	Open	Mar	20
Raja	Developer	Shankar	A1111	L	Open	Jan	140
Raja	Developer	Shankar	A1111	L	Open	Apr	160
Raja	Developer	Shankar	A1111	L	Open	May	100
Lisa	Developer	Jha	B2222	S	Open	Jan	150
Lisa	Developer	Jha	B2222	S	Open	Feb	120
Lisa	Developer	Jha	B2222	S	Open	Mar	130
Lisa	Developer	Jha	B2222	S	Open	Apr	100
Sonia	QA	Shankar	C3333	M	Open	Jan	80
Sonia	QA	Shankar	C3333	M	Open	Feb	80
Sonia	QA	Shankar	C3333	M	Open	Mar	120
Sonia	QA	Shankar	C3333	M	Open	Apr	120
Rita	Developer	Shankar	C3333	M	Open	May	40
Rita	Developer	Shankar	C3333	M	Open	Jan	150
Rita	Developer	Shankar	C3333	M	Open	Feb	150
Rita	Developer	Shankar	C3333	M	Open	Mar	150
Daisy	BA	Shankar	C3333	M	Open	Jan	120
Daisy	BA	Shankar	C3333	M	Open	Feb	120
Daisy	BA	Shankar	C3333	M	Open	Apr	120
Daisy	BA	Shankar	C3333	M	Open	May	120

Figure 4.14   Pivot: raw data 1.

Sum of Hrs allocated			Month					
Resource Name	Project Mgr	Project Number	Jan	Feb	Mar	Apr	May	Grand Total
Daisy	Shankar	C3333	120	120		120	120	480
	Shankar Total		120	120		120	120	480
Daisy Total			120	120		120	120	480
Donna	Jha	B2222	20	40	20		5	85
	Jha Total		20	40	20		5	85
Donna Total			20	40	20		5	85
Lisa	Jha	B2222	150	120	130	100		500
	Jha Total		150	120	130	100		500
Lisa Total			150	120	130	100		500
Mona	Jha	B2222	120	100	90	160	40	510
	Jha Total		120	100	90	160	40	510
	Shankar	A1111					120	120
	Shankar Total						120	120
Mona Total			120	100	90	160	160	630
Pam	Shankar	A1111	90			40		130
	Shankar Total		90			40		130
Pam Total			90			40		130

Raja	Shankar	A1111	140			160	100	400
	Shankar Total		140			160	100	400
Raja Total			140			160	100	400
Rita	Shankar	C3333	150	150	150		40	490
	Shankar Total		150	150	150		40	490
Rita Total			150	150	150		40	490
Sonia	Shankar	C3333	80	80	120	120		400
	Shankar Total		80	80	120	120		400
Sonia Total			80	80	120	120		400
Sunny	Jha	B2222					40	40
	Jha Total						40	40
	Shankar	A1111	20	160	150	140	120	590
	Shankar Total		20	160	150	140	120	590
Sunny Total			20	160	150	140	160	630
Grand Total			890	770	660	840	585	3745

Figure 4.15   Pivot table 1.

Date	Project	User	Activity	Deliverable	Hours
12/29/08	Proj 1	MALLADI,SONI	Integration and Testing	Del5000	1
12/29/08	Proj 1	MELVIN	Project Management	Del5000	2
12/29/08	Proj 1	MELVIN	Project Management	PPS	2
12/29/08	Proj 2	SONALI	Integration and Testing	Deliverable 2	2
12/29/08	Proj 2	SONALI	Technical Analysis	Deliverable 1	6
12/29/08	Proj 2	JOSEPH	Project Definition	Login Apps	1
12/29/08	Proj 2	JHA,SHANKAR	Project Management	1050 Release 2	2
12/29/08	Proj 2	JHA,SHANKAR	Project Management	Deliverable 2	2
12/29/08	Proj 2	JHA,SHANKAR	Project Management	Claim Audit	2
12/29/08	Proj 2	JHA,SHANKAR	Project Management	Daily 1050	2
12/29/08	Proj 2	RAM	Development and Construction	Deliverable 2	4
12/29/08	Proj 2	MICHAEL	Deployment	Deliverable 2	2
12/29/08	Proj 2	MICHAEL	Deployment	Daily 1050	4
12/29/08	Proj 2	MALLADI,SONI	Integration and Testing	Knowledge Transition	1
12/29/08	Proj 2	MURALI	Development and Construction	1050 Release 2	2
12/29/08	Proj 2	MURALI	Development and Construction	Claim Audit	2
12/29/08	Proj 2	MURALI	Development and Construction	PPS Parsing	2
12/29/08	Proj 2	MURALI	Development and Construction	Claim Extract	2
12/29/08	Proj 2	MELVIN	Project Management	Daily 1050	1
12/29/08	Proj 2	MELVIN	Project Management	Monthly 1050	2
12/29/08	Proj 2	MELVIN	Project Management	Deliverable 3	1
12/30/08	Proj 1	RAM	Deployment	Del5000	4
12/30/08	Proj 1	MALLADI,SONI	Integration and Testing	Del5000	1
12/30/08	Proj 1	MELVIN	Project Management	Del5000	2
12/30/08	Proj 1	MELVIN	Project Management	PPS	1
12/30/08	Proj 1	MELVIN	Project Management	Contribution Automation	1
12/30/08	Proj 1	MELVIN	Project Management	Contribution Automation	1
12/30/08	Proj 2	SONALI	Integration and Testing	Deliverable 2	3

12/30/08	Proj 2	SONALI	Technical Analysis	Deliverable 1	5
12/30/08	Proj 2	JOSEPH	Project Definition	Deliverable 1	1
12/30/08	Proj 2	JHA,SHANKAR	Project Management	1050 Release 2	2
12/30/08	Proj 2	JHA,SHANKAR	Project Management	Deliverable 2	2
12/30/08	Proj 2	JHA,SHANKAR	Project Management	Claim Audit	2
12/30/08	Proj 2	JHA,SHANKAR	Project Management	Daily 1050	2
12/30/08	Proj 2	RAM	Development and Construction	Deliverable 2	4
12/30/08	Proj 2	MICHAEL	Deployment	Deliverable 2	2
12/30/08	Proj 2	MICHAEL	Deployment	Daily 1050	4
12/30/08	Proj 2	MALLADI,SONI	Integration and Testing	Knowledge Transition	1
12/30/08	Proj 2	MURALI	Development and Construction	1050 Release 2	2
12/30/08	Proj 2	MURALI	Development and Construction	Claim Audit	2
12/30/08	Proj 2	MURALI	Development and Construction	PPS Parsing	2
12/30/08	Proj 2	MURALI	Development and Construction	Claim Extract	2
12/30/08	Proj 2	MELVIN	Project Management	Daily 1050	2
12/30/08	Proj 2	MELVIN	Project Management	Monthly 1050	1
12/31/08	Proj 1	MALLADI,SONI	Integration and Testing	Del5000	1
12/31/08	Proj 1	MELVIN	Project Management	Del5000	2
12/31/08	Proj 2	SONALI	Integration and Testing	Deliverable 2	3
12/31/08	Proj 2	SONALI	Technical Analysis	Deliverable 1	5
12/31/08	Proj 2	JHA,SHANKAR	Project Management	1050 Release 2	2
12/31/08	Proj 2	JHA,SHANKAR	Project Management	Deliverable 2	2
12/31/08	Proj 2	JHA,SHANKAR	Project Management	Claim Audit	2
12/31/08	Proj 2	JHA,SHANKAR	Project Management	Daily 1050	2
12/31/08	Proj 2	RAM	Deployment	Daily/Monthly 1050	6
12/31/08	Proj 2	MICHAEL	Deployment	Deliverable 2	2

Figure 4.16   Pivot: raw data 2.

—continued

Date	Project	User	Activity	Deliverable	Hours
12/31/08	Proj 2	MICHAEL	Deployment	Daily 1050	4
12/31/08	Proj 2	MALLADI,SONI	Integration and Testing	Knowledge Transition	1
12/31/08	Proj 2	MURALI	Development and Construction	1050 Release 2	2
12/31/08	Proj 2	MURALI	Development and Construction	Claim Audit	2
12/31/08	Proj 2	MURALI	Development and Construction	PPS Parsing	2
12/31/08	Proj 2	MURALI	Development and Construction	Claim Extract	2
12/31/08	Proj 2	MELVIN	Project Management	Claim Audit	2
12/31/08	Proj 2	MELVIN	Project Management	Daily 1050	2
12/31/08	Proj 2	MELVIN	Project Management	Monthly 1050	1
12/31/08	Proj 2	MELVIN	Project Management	Deliverable 3	1
1/2/09	Proj 1	RAM	Deployment	Del5000	2
1/2/09	Proj 1	MELVIN	Project Management	Contribution Automation	2
1/2/09	Proj 1	MELVIN	Project Management	Contribution Automation	2
1/2/09	Proj 2	SONALI	Integration and Testing	Deliverable 2	3
1/2/09	Proj 2	SONALI	Technical Analysis	Deliverable 1	5
1/2/09	Proj 2	JHA,SHANKAR	Project Management	1050 Release 2	2
1/2/09	Proj 2	JHA,SHANKAR	Project Management	Deliverable 2	2
1/2/09	Proj 2	JHA,SHANKAR	Project Management	Claim Audit	2
1/2/09	Proj 2	JHA,SHANKAR	Project Management	Daily 1050	2
1/2/09	Proj 2	RAM	Deployment	Daily/Monthly 1050	4
1/2/09	Proj 2	MURALI	Development and Construction	1050 Release 2	2
1/2/09	Proj 2	MURALI	Development and Construction	Claim Audit	2
1/2/09	Proj 2	MURALI	Development and Construction	PPS Parsing	2
1/2/09	Proj 2	MURALI	Development and Construction	Claim Extract	2
1/2/09	Proj 2	MELVIN	Project Management	PPS	2
1/2/09	Proj 2	MELVIN	Project Management	Deliverable 3	2

Figure 4.16 (continued)   Pivot: raw data 2.

Sum of Hours			Project		
User	Activity	Deliverable	Proj 1	Proj 2	Grand Total
JHA,SHANKAR	Project Management	1050 Release 2		8	8
		Claim Audit		8	8
		Daily 1050		8	8
		Deliverable 2		8	8
	Project Management Total			32	32
JHA,SHANKAR Total				32	32
JOSEPH	Project Definition	Deliverable 1		1	1
		Login Apps		1	1
	Project Definition Total			2	2
JOSEPH Total				2	2
MALLADI,SONI	Integration and Testing	Del5000	3		3
		Knowledge Transition		3	3
	Integration and Testing Total		3	3	6
MALLADI,SONI Total			3	3	6

Figurre 4.17 Pivot table 2.

—continued

Resource	Category	Task			
MELVIN	Project Management	Claim Audit		2	2
		Contribution Automation	5		5
		Daily 1050		5	5
		Del5000	6		6
		Deliverable 3		4	4
		Member Contribution Automation	1		1
		Monthly 1050		4	4
		PPS	3	2	5
	Project Management Total		15	17	32
MELVIN Total			15	17	32
MICHAEL	Deployment	Daily 1050		12	12
		Deliverable 2		6	6
	Deployment Total			18	18
MICHAEL Total				18	18
MURALI	Development and Construction	1050 Release 2		8	8
		Claim Audit		8	8
		Claim Extract		8	8
		PPS parsing		8	8
	Development and Construction Total			32	32
MURALI Total				32	32
RAM	Deployment	daily/monthly 1050		10	10
		Del5000	6		6
	Deployment Total		6	10	16
	Development and Construction	Deliverable 2		8	8

Development and Construction Total			8	8
RAM Total		6	18	24
SONALI	Deliverable 2		11	11
Integration and Testing Total			11	11
	Deliverable 1		21	21
Technical Analysis			21	21
Technical Analysis Total			32	32
SONALI Total			154	178
Grand Total		24		

Figure 4.17 (continued) Pivot table 2.

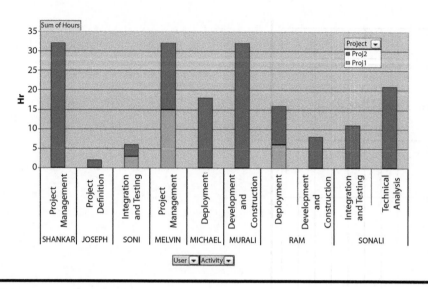

Figure 4   Pivot chart.

Chapter 5

Conclusion and Case Studies

Is project management a science or an art? Arguably, it is more of a science. At the same time, there is quite a bit of art involved in this profession. Because communication is such an important part of the entire project management process, communication management is also as much a science as it is an art. Templates, guidelines, standards, etc., along with the documented process, constitute the science part, but how the project managers (PMs) use these tools with the help of their behavioral traits is pure art. The element of science ensures that the use of previously experimented tools and established processes provides predictable results. The art element provides freedom to exercise creativity and bring individuality under the limits of the process. Knowing the science is essential, but one cannot afford to ignore the art of communication, which applies to all three components—that is, verbal, nonverbal, and written. The art of communication reminds me of a very interesting and inspiring story that goes as follows.

> Akbar, a Mogul Emperor, was the most influential and successful king in medieval history of India (later his grandson built the famous Taj Mahal). He himself was illiterate, but he had nine very bright and learned courtiers famously known as the "nine jewels of the Mogul Crown." Among all the courtiers, Birbal was the most popular, witty, and intelligent. For this reason, Akbar, the king, liked Birbal the most. One night, Akbar had a bad dream that all his teeth had fallen out except one. In the

morning he invited all the astrologers into his court and asked them to interpret the dream. Astrologers had a long meeting and at last they all reached the conclusion that it meant that all of his relatives would die before him. So, they said the same to Akbar. Hearing this, Akbar felt very bad and became concerned about his relatives. He sent all the astrologers away without giving prizes. He was frightened. The entire day passed in restlessness. In the evening, Birbal came. Akbar told his dream to Birbal and asked him to interpret it. Birbal thought for a minute, smiled, and said, "My Lord, this means that you will live a longer and more-fulfilled life than any of your relatives." Akbar was very pleased and he rewarded him heavily.

Essentially, both the astrologers and Birbal interpreted the dream in a similar manner, but the difference was in communication and hence the reward that it fetched. So remember to bring in both elements (science and art) into practice while trying to respond to any situation of communication management.

Project managers face testing times throughout almost the entire project—in particular, the planning process in the early phases of the project and the monitoring and control process in the later phases are the most challenging. Note that the planning process is different from the planning phase. The planning process along with most of the other project management processes (initiating, planning, execution, monitoring and control, and closing) is repeated in every phase of the project. The name of the phase and the number of project phases vary from organization to organization, but the project processes are the same in each project. Project managers own so many documents in the planning phase that people generally become confused about what documents to create and in which sequence to create them. If an organization has a sound project management process in place, one can cruise through this phase comparatively smoothly, but no process defines a framework for how you would react in a crisis situation. Chapter 2 provided an idea of the planning documents, their contents, and the sequence in which they are created. Chapter 3 explained some helpful tools that one can use to "weather the storm" during a crisis.

It is not a matter of *if* the challenges will occur; it is *when* they will occur. But then again, "smooth seas do not make skillful sailors." One can sail through the waves of these challenges with the use of appropriate communication tools and tips. The possibilities are endless; one should use the resources (tools in this case) as per the demand of the situation. Some typical challenging situations for project managers are listed below; I am sure you will have a sense of déjà vu. Answers are not provided so that readers are provoked to think and hence they become better prepared for the real-life situations. Albert Einstein has said, "Imagination is more important than knowledge." One will face many other kinds of challenges, which no one can predict, but if one has sound fundamental knowledge, an open mind, and positive thinking, then he/she can overcome any challenge that the profession of project management presents. Keep an open mind while approaching the resolution of conflicts. Look at the problem from different angles; as Abraham Maslow says, "If the only tool you have is a hammer, you tend to see every problem as a nail." This means that every interest group will approach the problem from their respective angles—business users will look at the problem from a business perspective, technical persona will see the problem technically, but you, as a project manager, are the one who must have a comprehensive view.

The scenarios below have been categorized based on the categorization of the chapters in this book. Try to come up with a resolution to these problems based on your experience and the reading of this book.

Scenarios on the Usage of Text-Based Tools

1. **Unknown and Unplanned Event:** You are the PM of a multimillion-dollar, high-visibility software development project. As a PM you prepared a project plan after taking input from all key stakeholders and team members. The plan has received due approval. Everyone happily starts working toward the goal of finishing the design and construction work. The design documentation finishes on time, all the reviews take place, design is signed off, and project is still on track by the end of the design phase. Midway through the construction, your technical lead shares some bad news: There is a major flaw in the design of one of the critical and largest pieces. He proposes the need for analyzing the components again, redesigning, and then doing the rework on construction of that piece. The project already has resource crunch. You know that business will not agree to postpone the implementation date by a single day, and you also know that the project sponsor will not spend a single penny extra because of the budget cuts in the portfolio.

   Issues to Examine: What will be your first reaction? What you will do next? How you will break this news to the business owner and sponsor? What suggestions will you make?

2. **Structured Agenda for Better Meeting Results:** You are the PM of an IT project. Functional testing is over and while doing regression testing, QA testers have logged a critical defect. They found that the new data looks good but part of the old data is broken. You consult the technical lead and the lead business analyst, who suggest a few options, but they are not very confident about those options. The resolution they suggest is a stop-gap arrangement.

   Issues to Examine: What would be your next steps from a communication management perspective? Present a layout of the agenda of the most critical meeting that you would conduct to resolve the problem.

3. Premature Termination: You are managing a project to support a new product that your organization plans to launch at the beginning of next year. The project is in GREEN status and everything is going well. One fine morning you see an email from the business owner/sponsor to stop all work on the project. The project must be put on hold indefinitely because the company has decided to delay the product launch due to changes in the market situation.

Issues to Examine: What should be done to handle this situation from a communication management perspective? List all the steps and provide details of the communication tools you will use.

4. Recalcitrant Customer: Your project involves interaction with three different customer organizations, one of which, say organization X, is the major user of the product this project is creating. The directors of these customer organizations are members of the project steering committee. You conduct the steering committee meeting on a monthly basis, but somehow no representative of organization X shows up at any of the three steering committee meetings you have had. First meeting: Director X declines the meeting just when the meeting started. Second meeting: Director X declines a day before the meeting and informs you that someone else will represent organization X at the meeting. You do not hear from the other person and the meeting takes place without any representation from organization X. Third meeting: You approach Director X and explain why it is necessary for him or his organization to be represented at the meeting for the success of the project—because a major decision must be made with agreement from all three customers. You have made sure that the meeting time is convenient for all participants and they have accepted the invitation. Unfortunately, organization X remains unrepresented once again. This is affecting project progress, as decisions are not being made on time.

Issues to Examine: Discuss the communication tools, along with their major contents, that you will use to sort out this communication problem.

5. Progress Report: There is a regular weekly project review meeting with the organization's senior management for all the major projects being executed in the portfolio. They generally discuss the status of the projects and review schedule, cost, risk, and issues. Your project is one of the twenty-odd projects that will be reviewed.

Issues to Examine: What documents/reports would you distribute to the participants before the meeting?

6. Where Is the Project Plan?: Your project started about a month ago and so far you have sent out the project initiation document to the team, completed the project plan (review and signoff process is in progress), and currently you are working on the preparation of a project kickoff meeting, which will be held in a week's time. There have been few meetings with project team members and the customers during this period. Core team members are working on the project; however, a detailed schedule is not ready yet for obvious reasons. In fact, dates for some interim milestones are also not very clear at this time. Some team members are raising concerns that the project is moving without a project plan (yes, they say that there is no project plan) and they have complained about this to their respective resource managers.

Issues to Examine: Discuss (1) what might be the reason behind such complaints by some of the project team members; (2) how you would explain the difference between project plan and project schedule, and (3) how you would explain why the schedule is not yet ready.

7. **The Triple Constraint:** In your multimillion-dollar project, you find that the timelines are too tight to implement the project with existing resources. Hence, you have flagged the project to YELLOW status. You approach senior management in this regard, stating the risk of schedule slippage, and you present some options, such as (1) approval to increase the budget so that more workers can be acquired to expedite the work; (2) if more workers are not available, then existing labor can work overtime to finish the work faster; and (3) change the timelines. Unfortunately, none of these options are approved.

Issues to Examine: What would you do next to bring the project to GREEN status? [Hint: Remember the triple constraints of cost, scope, and time.]

8. **Poorly Defined Scope or Quality Mismanagement:** A software development project is in the user acceptance testing (UAT) phase. The project is being executed using waterfall methodology. This project will integrate data from a couple of legacy systems into the enterprise data warehouse of the company. As a good PM, you have acquired all the required signoffs internally as well as from the customers for all the major deliverables. However, during UAT, after looking at the first set of data, the customers report major defects that will require major changes in the requirements and the design. Your organization states that it has conformed to the requirements signed off by the customer. However, the customers argue that this is not fit for their use. They did not understand the requirements document completely and were not very confident until they saw the live data. The cost of the changes will be more than double the original project cost and will stretch the timeline for a considerable time period.

Issues to Examine: It is obvious from the scenario that the customers do not have a clear idea about the details they need in the requirements. UAT is the second-last phase of the project, so the need for such a major rework was uncovered very late in the project. Did this situation arise because the project followed waterfall methodology? If yes, then which methodology should the project have followed to avoid this situation? What else, from a communication management perspective, might have caused this issue? Analyze the situation and draw up the next steps and future strategies for the project.

9. **Get Ready to Wear that Creative Hat:** There is no formal configuration control process in the organization. It is practiced in bits and pieces. There is no audit to ensure that everyone properly follows the process. You are very well aware of the benefits of the configuration management processes. It is not possible to formulate and implement the process overnight throughout the organization. But you want to initiate the best practice for others to benchmark and follow. You have very limited resources and bandwidth in the project to do so,

and additionally you will not get additional support from outside. From your experience with previous projects in this organization, you have collected data about issues and rework resulting from noncompliance with configuration control practices. Some of the major areas of improvement are (1) improper version control of the critical documents, leading to confusion, conflict, and rework; and (2) a lack of awareness on the part of the project team about project folder structure. Because of this, documents are stored all over the place and the documents are seldom stored in the right place.

Issues to Examine: Assuming you will not get the budget for acquiring a full-fledged configuration control tool and you will not get an outside auditor for monitoring the configuration control work on the project, what should you do to ensure tackling the above-mentioned problems with minimal fuss?

10. **Knowledge Management in a Project? Uhh:** For some reason, there is very high turnover in your organization. This is a known risk, and one that you are aware of. Historically, there have been many issues in some recent projects. The projects have failed to complete on time and within budget for this reason. There have also been comparatively more customer complaints of late. So, you identify this as one of the very high priority risks and document it accordingly in the project risk register. One of the risk responses to mitigate the risk impact is to follow knowledge management (KM) practice in the project.

Issues to Examine: List the best practices that you can follow to do a formal knowledge management exercise. What should you do to ensure that the budget and resources are allocated sufficiently to carry out the formal KM activities in the project? Which communication documents/tools would you use, apart from adding KM as a task in the project schedule?

11. **Information Overdose versus Information Scarcity:** You are managing a software development project. In one of the project status meetings, you hear complaints from a group of team members (database administrators and architects) that they are not being copied on all project emails. They argue that they do not get first-hand information and thus do not feel that they are part of the project. You try to reason with them, explaining that you do not want people to get overwhelmed with every email that may not be related to their work. Their point is that the tech lead and business analyst are kept informed about everything on the project but that these team members do not get most of the information directly about the issues and events regarding the project. And although every email may not be related to their work, they feel that receiving every email will help because they will be kept informed. They get very emotional about this and state that they feel they have been left out on occasion. This argument sidetracks the main agenda of the project meeting and things seem to get more heated. The more you try to convince them, the more agitated they appear.

Issues to Examine: What should you do to stop the argument from stretching further and to achieve the objectives of the status meeting? How should you tackle the concerns of this section of project team members? The last thing you want is to let the morale of the team go down and at the same time you also understand the benefits of effective and efficient communication as well as the impacts of information overload. How would you keep this balance intact?

12. **Oh, No. I Forgot to Work on This With Too Many Things Going on:**
    You need to do a lot of follow-ups in your new project. Topics are discussed
    in different meetings and next steps are decided; but to your disappoint-
    ment, seldom are they addressed on time. You need to remind people about
    their action items and only then do they work on it. This impacts progress
    and adds unnecessary work for you.

    Issues to Examine: What may be lacking from the communication process
    perspective? Suggest some best communication practices so that team mem-
    bers do not have to be reminded by the PM about their action items.

13. **I Hate Change Requests:** You are at the end of the planning phase of the
    project. Core project team members have performed an initial analysis of
    the project scope. You have asked the leads and the experts to provide a
    high-level estimate of the project cost based on their analysis. The project
    has an approved budget of $2.0 million. The estimates provided by the
    experts indicate that the estimate at completion (EAC) will be in the range
    of $3.5 million to $4.5 million. You ask the team to mention assumptions
    that they considered while doing the estimation because you understand
    that no planning and estimation should be done without listing assump-
    tions. When the assumptions fail, they turn into risks and issues. These
    assumptions are validated against the assumptions mentioned in the project
    charter. It is found that some of the assumptions listed in the charter do not
    "hold water." This is one of the main reasons why the project cost estimate
    is double the approved budget. You document and submit a change control
    for extra budget; but because of a freeze on any extra financial expenditure
    in the portfolio, the change control is rejected.

    Issues to Examine: How should you handle the situation to keep the project
    moving forward? The project cannot be stopped or scrapped, and at the same
    time you cannot continue toward burning anything more than $2.0 million on
    this project. Would you submit another change control? If yes, then what should
    that be for?

14. **Baseline and Variation Tolerance:** In the above scenario, you collect the
    estimates from all the functional leads and then sum them to calculate the
    total estimate (E2) for the project. The new estimate at completion (EAC)
    is approximately 20 percent more than the OOM estimate (E1).

    Issues to Examine: The project sponsor asks you to submit a change control for
    the increased cost. However, as per the industry standards, you know that final
    estimates may vary by 50 percent to 100 percent of the OOM. Your organization
    has not formally defined any such variation limits for the estimations, nor does
    the project management plan elaborately capture any guidelines for project esti-
    mation and cost baseline for the project. People generally consider the estimates
    as the final figure without any tolerance for variation, no matter at what stage
    the estimation was done. **Should you submit the change control? If not, then
    how would you convince the project sponsor?** You understand that estimation
    needs to be performed again after the design is complete and the tolerance limit
    for that final estimate (E3) would be ±10 percent. This means that, at any point
    after the third estimation (E3), if you have a sense that the final actual cost will
    exceed more than 10 percent of E3, or will be less than 10 percent of the E3, then
    you need to try to bring the cost into the ±10 percent range. In case that is not

possible, then write a change control to get approval for the new budget, which will then be considered the new baseline.

15. **Communication Breakdown Invites Issues:** You are the PM of a project that supports information technology (IT) solutions for a Medicaid plan for the members in a particular state. Because the state government owns the health-care plan, your organization has a regulatory obligation to the state apart from the contractual obligations for many project deliverables. The project has a matrix organization. You have followed all the standard project processes of the organization in delivering the products and services to the state. The state reports a major defect in one of the critical deliverables. You are asked to fix the defect and reproduce the deliverable within one month, failing which your company will have to pay a severe penalty to the state. You consult your supervisor and report the issue to her. You are very concerned that the fix will require a significant change that will require a lot of time and cost. The cost performance index of the project does not show a healthy sign, so you also want to be careful with the project cost. You understand the system and the business very well. To save time and cost and meet the state's requirements, you get creative and suggest that the fix be done using a semi-manual workaround because the deliverable is of a temporary nature. This semi-manual workaround is quick and does not need much IT development. Your supervisor likes the idea, and so does the business owner of the project. So, you get the issue resolved within the stipulated time frame without spending much for the fix and feel very proud of it. However, after about a month, the client reports another big issue regarding the same deliverable, but a deliverable that does not have a manual or semi-manual workaround. You need a development resource immediately to fix the defect. This time you approach the IT development head, requesting him to give you a resource immediately. Before committing the resource, the development head inquires about the background of the issue and he becomes aware of the prior semi-manual workaround done outside the IT development framework. He becomes very upset about that and complains that he was not kept informed about the decision of the prior workaround. He argues that not following proper IT processes leads to such failure points and the work was done outside the purview of architectural considerations and SOX (Sarbanes–Oxley) checkpoints. The development head then escalates this situation to the senior management level.

Issues to Examine: Should the development head have been informed about the decision of the semi-manual workaround? Why should the development unit be so worried when the business was ready to take the risk and had agreed to the semi-manual workaround? Is this a case of communication breakdown? Should you take the matter in your own hands to meet the deadlines, or should you reach out to all the major stakeholders of your company for a collaborative decision?

16. **Smart Communicator Is the Best Negotiator:** Obtaining approval can be very challenging at times and may lead to friction, schedule slippage, cost overruns, and customer dissatisfaction. The PM's communication skills are tested in such circumstances and a lot depends on how the PM communicates with the approver and how the matter is escalated. On many occasions, the deliverables are unduly kept on hold, and the approver complicates the matter by adding too many unreasonable conditions.

Persuasion and communication skills of the PM light the path to conflict resolution in such circumstances. It is critical that the PM appropriately presents the facts, the impact of delay to future deliverables, and to overall project health. Escalation through the proper channels and involvement of the right people always prove fruitful.

The key customers of your IT project are very difficult to work with; they are unprofessional as well as uncooperative. Your organization is a subcontractor for the project in such a way that your company has a contract with company A, whereas company A is the primary contractor for company B. So, company B is an indirect customer of your company. According to the contract, all the project deliverables require signoff from company A only. You cannot approach company B directly; you will have to approach B through A. For various reasons, the requirements for one of the deliverables are not signed off on time by company A. They argue that they want to see the data and only then will they sign off. The project proceeds with the design and development work, based on the requirements documented. The data is produced and sent to company A for review. Upon review of the data, company A reports many major issues. You have multiple meetings with the subject matter experts from both sides to understand the issues. All the issues are documented properly and the data is fixed; but upon reviewing the result, they report some new issues. These issues were present also in the old data, but company A did not perform a thorough review and verification, and did not catch these issues the first time. In the meantime, you keep pressing them for signoff but they keep arguing that because the data was not fixed properly, they will not sign off. This matter is escalated but does not bear any result. As time passes, the deadline set by company B for the deliverable passes, which impacts their business, so company B becomes upset and threatens to take the matter to court.

Issues to Examine: In this scenario, what should have been done to avoid the situation getting to the level where it is now? How would you handle the current situation? What is the root cause of the problem?

17. **Callous Senior Management:** The project kickoff meeting is a very important meeting for the project. Understanding that this is your first opportunity as a PM in a new organization to make an impression, you have prepared very well for this meeting. The kickoff meeting sets the tone for the rest of the project. But unfortunately, many key stakeholders do not show up to the meeting and do not even inform you—however, everyone had accepted the invitation. You wait for ten minutes in the meeting with some participants and then you call off the meeting because there is no point in going forward without most of the key stakeholders present. It is very difficult to get a timeslot together in the calendars of senior executives again. So you feel very frustrated about this. And being new to the organization, you do not understand the culture of this organization very well.

Issues to Examine: How should you react to this callous attitude of the executives toward such an important project meeting? Prepare a list of steps the PM should take to handle the situation in such a way that he/she gets the job done without showing any kind of frustration and at the same time wins everyone's heart.

Scenarios on the Usage of Chart-, Graph-, and Diagram-Based Tools

18. **Problem-Solving Tool:** Your multimillion-dollar project, which was supposed to finish in a total of twenty-four months, is abruptly coming to a premature halt. This project was planned to commission, in two phases, two high-capacity, state-of-the-art steel melting shops for a young but promising steel maker ABC Inc. Your organization, XYZ Inc., has signed a contract with ABC Inc. on a Build-Operate-Transfer (BOT) basis. As per the contract, after the end of the project, XYZ Inc. will support the operations for next ten years and will receive a service charge at per-million tons of steel production per quarter. After fourteen months, XYZ Inc. realizes that it is not a good investment, considering the current and future market conditions. Instead, if it invests in some other project, it will get much better returns. Apart from the financial facts, ABC Inc. has not been a very good business partner on many fronts. So, XYZ decides to pay the penalty according to the contract terms and get out of the business with ABC, Inc.

    One of the steel melting shops is already commissioned and production started last month; XYZ is operating and maintaining this shop. As per the terms of contract terminations, XYZ must continue the steel production operations from shop one, as well as the factory installation work for shop two, for at least seven months after XYZ signs the contract termination agreement. This is to ensure that the customers and vendors of ABC are not impacted by any transition or termination. Because XYZ is exiting the contract, it wants to spend as little on the project and the operation as possible yet support the customer and vendor. Before the termination was decided, XYZ had planned to use high-tech machines and tools. But in the current situation, senior management of XYZ is exploring options to carry out as many tasks using manual and semi-manual means as possible without doing any further investment. Use of high-tech machines and tools requires a significant investment and skilled man power, which is of no use because of XYZ's departure from the project.

    You have been asked by senior management to prepare a list of major remaining project activities that are planned for the next seven months, as well as the cost to finish those activities. Next, you need to identify manual and semi-manual options for every activity. Additionally, a cost comparison of manual versus automated solution is also required. You have also been asked to lay out a plan to carry out the transition/close-out activities.

    Issues to Examine: What communication tool would you use to manage the transition? Understanding the intention of senior management and considering the financial interest of your organization, you would like to separate out the large cost-saving items from the small cost-saving items in order to reap the maximum benefit of manual operation. You are planning to list all the remaining scope items as advised by the senior management and then prepare a matrix for the automation cost, manual cost, and savings against each item. What tool would you use to separate the vital few items from the trivial many? How would you collect all the data? Analyze the situation and list steps to carry out the entire exercise in line with the expectations of senior management.

19. **What Is the Option?:** You are working as a PM for a construction company. The company has signed a deal for constructing roads and flyovers in a particular state. The company does not have enough spare machinery to engage in this new project, so it must either purchase or rent the machinery for the duration of the project. You have been asked by senior management to come up with a decision as to whether to purchase or rent the machinery. The decision should give the best value for the money invested. You also need to document and present to senior management the reasoning behind the decision. As a next step, you set up a meeting of experts to collect input. You also interview many people offline to record relevant information that needs to be factored into the decision-making process. The cost of purchase is $10 million. If you purchase from an existing vendor, the chance of payoff is 70 percent, with the net payoff being $15 million. If the purchase is made from a new vendor, the chance of payoff is 30 percent, with the net payoff being $18 million. At the same time, the cost of renting is $6 million. If the machinery is rented from an existing vendor, then the chance of payoff is 60 percent, with the net payoff being $10 million. The chance of payoff is 40 percent when the machinery is rented from a new vendor, with the pay-off being $6 million.

Issues to Examine: Which tool would you use for making this decision and for presenting your case to senior management? Document how the tool was used to arrive at the conclusion.

Scenarios on the Usage of Tables and Matrix-Based Tools

20. **Communicaiton Consistency:** The head of your PMO (Project Management Office) organization has been asked by the CIO to present the status of all critical projects being executed in the PMO. Your project is one of them. The status meeting is scheduled at 1:00 p.m. every Monday, so the PMO head asks every concerned PM to send her a brief summary status of critical project parameters by 8:00 a.m. every Monday morning. Thus, she can have enough time to review the status and ask individual PMs for more details before the meeting, if required. In one of the regular PMO meetings, the PMO head expresses concern that some of the reports have extra details, while some have many fewer details. Apart from that, she is asking for suggestions to make this process dynamic so that she can obtain the information anytime for any project, irrespective of whether or not the project manager is in the office.

Issues to Examine: What process improvement would you suggest to make life easy for the PMO head and the project managers? Which communication tool can make the critical project data available anytime for anyone?

21. **Dispel the Cloud of Confusion:** Your project is in the requirements analysis phase and is overstaying in this phase for a little more than two weeks. You go on vacation for two weeks and upon return find that the project has not made much progress during the two weeks you were away. The requirements analysis was supposed to finish during the week before you left, but could not finish because of some issues. Before leaving for the vacation, you conducted a meeting with all the stakeholders, including the analyst. The next steps were discussed and it was expected that the analysis would finish in the next two days. But to your dismay, upon your return, nobody is very sure about the number of issues, who is responsible for closing them, the expected turnaround (ETA), etc. Everything is either documented through email or was discussed in the meetings, which is in people's minds.
Issues to Examine: From a communication process perspective, what do you think is the root cause of the delay in finishing the requirements analysis phase? As a PM, are you responsible for the lapse in communication even though you were out of the action for two weeks? What should be the next step for the PM? What should be done to prevent such things from happening again?

22. **Who Is Responsible? I'm Not:** You are the PM of a construction project. The designer has completed the design. He notifies you about the completion of the artifact. When you ask him if this artifact is verified and approved, he responds that he does not know who will verify and approve the design. You tell the designer the names of people (customer, architect, electrical engineer, plumbing lead, etc.) to whom he should send the design and you also ask him that the review, rework, and approval be completed in one week as not much time is left. Later you hear that some of the recipients/approvers respond back, saying that (1) they do not know if they are the right people to review the design; and (2) not enough notice/time was given, so they cannot finish the review in the specified time frame.
Issues to Examine: From a communication management perspective, what lapses have occurred here? You realize that it is better late than never, so you decide to fix the communication process. What communication tools would you prepare and distribute to preclude this situation from going forward? [Hint: The project schedule is not the only tool to be used in this situation.]

23. **Prepare a List, Prevent a Leak:** This is the end of the design phase and you hold a phase gate review meeting with all the project stakeholders. The customers raise a concern that they did not get two of the deliverables that were supposed to finish by the end of the design phase. You realize that they are big deliverables and will require at least four weeks of time to finish. This will impact the project timelines. You did not know that the project was supposed to produce those deliverables. One of the customers stated that this was communicated to one of the VPs of your company in an email a long time ago when the project was in the proposal phase. The VP acknowledges that the email was received, but somehow it was never documented in any of the scope documents and nobody realized this until now. You cannot propose a change request for this because you never prepared a list of deliverables, so the customer never got a chance to review and approve.
Issues to Examine: You cannot change what has already happened, but you do want to cure the process going forward. What documents would you prepare,

update, and/or obtain signoff on from the customers and other stakeholders? In other words, what communication tools would you use to prevent similar mishaps in the future?

24. **Communication Gap in Responsibility Assignment:** You join an NGO (non-governmental organization) to work with another PM on a social development project that is in progress. The WBS for your part of the project is already complete. However, you are not sure about all the resources that should be associated with various activities. The activities of the project need to be performed collaboratively with the help of several labor groups and experts from inside and outside the project team. Upon inquiring of the existing PM and other team members, you come to know about the resources responsible for carrying out the various project work, but you are not sure which group will provide technical insight on the different tasks, who will own the work, and who you should keep apprised of all the developments. You hear that the other PM is also facing similar problems for most of her tasks. This is affecting the work of the project as you do not understand whom you should approach for all the activities. Some team members have also joined the project recently and are also facing similar problems in carrying out their day-to-day work.

Issues to Examine: What communication tool should you create and use in the project to overcome this problem? How would you create it? [Hint: The project schedule cannot provide answers to all of the issues stated above.]

25. **Role, Responsibility, Skill Set:** You need five extra software engineers for a period of four months on your project that starts two months from now, so you give a heads-up to the development manager. Unfortunately, there is no staff available in the department during the time you need them; all are allocated to other critical and strategic assignments. Your project cannot be stopped because of its business criticality. So, the required software engineers need to be hired from outside on a contract basis. You want to post the advertisement on some job search websites. You understand the responsibilities for these roles but you are not sure about the necessary competencies of these resources. This information is required before any advertisement can be placed.

Issues to Examine: Which tool would provide the information you are looking for? If the tool is not ready, then who should prepare the tool and who should participate in the process?

26. **Too Many Reports:** There is a transition of PM in a project, where you are replacing the existing PM. The transition takes place in less than a week, and you have tried to capture as much information as possible about the project and the organization. After a few days, you realize that various stakeholders are expecting multiple reports from you at different frequencies and there is no consistency in their demands. Being new to the organization, you do not understand every aspect of the process of the organization and at the same time you do not want to hurt anyone. In the process, you end up overspending your valuable time working on these demands and do not find enough time for carrying out your other day-to-day project work. Despite this, not everyone is happy because the expectations are not set properly.

Issues to Examine: Which communication tool should you use to set the expectations of the stakeholders? You want to make sure that everybody receives sufficient information about the project as per their genuine needs. The tool should have information about all the communication needs of all key stakeholders, mode of communication, frequency of communication, etc.

Miscellaneous Scenarios on the Usage of More than One Category of Tools

27. **One-on-One with a Senior Executive:** You are the PM of a critical project, which has been in YELLOW status (mainly because of schedule slippages) for a month and you are planning to report it as RED in your next status report. Your organization gets a new senior VP, who in his second week in his new office goes through the status of all critical projects in one of the executive meetings. Just after that meeting, he sends a note to you and the PMO Director and asks you to schedule a thirty-minute project review meeting with him. He wants to know in detail why the project is in YELLOW status and what can be done to bring it back to GREEN.
Issues to Examine: How will you respond to this situation? What plans, reports, and documents would you bring to the meeting?

28. **Panic in Project:** Organization A has bagged a very big contract to develop an IT system for a new healthcare plan for the state government. The project is scheduled to finish in eight months. Five months into the project, the executive leadership realizes that there is no way the project can finish in the committed time frame. Organization A risks sanctions and penalties if it fails to implement the business functionalities on time. The situation is so bad that some of the components already delivered to the state were rejected, stating quality reasons. Looking into the reasons why the deliveries were rejected, it was found that proper signoffs were not received on the business requirements and so there are open and gray areas that are the causes of contention. Proper project management processes were not followed and escalations were not made appropriately to bring senior management's attention to them on time. Panicked by the situation, the existing PM is released and you are assigned to the job because you are one of the most respected PMs in the organization. There is a lot of confusion between the project team and the business unit regarding the business needs and IT deliverables. Risks and issues are not being tracked and escalated properly.
Issues to Examine: How would you approach the situation? Lay out a plan to rescue the project and bring sanity to the project.

29. **Resolve the Dispute:** On the software development project you are managing, two of the key team members, the lead business analyst (BA) and the tech lead, do not get along very well. They always fight with each other. The project is in the testing phase and a critical defect has been detected by QA. The project is already behind schedule for the current phase and there is tremendous pressure from the customer to finish the project on time. The

tech lead argues that the programs have already changed many times for the requirement defects. He suggests that before changing the program further for the current defect, the BA should consult business experts and elaborate the requirements document to include all possible scenarios. The BA argues that these are all design and technical issues, which a BA cannot understand, and such details cannot be put into the requirements document. By the way, none of these resources report to you directly; they report to their respective functional managers.

Issues to Examine: Analyze the root cause of the conflict and what you would tell/instruct the BA and the tech lead in order to resolve the conflict. In case you are still unable to resolve the conflict, what should your next steps be?

30. **Managing Disputes:** A software project started more than three months ago. The PM had a rough order of magnitude (ROM) estimate at the beginning of the project, which appears to be significantly underestimated. Project completion was planned for six months; however, four months into the project, it is still in the design phase. Considering the size of the scope and the complexity of functionalities, it appears very unlikely that the project would even finish in seven months. Requirements analysis was completed toward the end of third month. The development lead and development manager, along with the QA lead, attended the requirements gathering discussions and also participated in thorough requirements document walkthrough sessions. Business users signed off on the requirements before that phase officially ended. Three weeks have gone by since the completion of requirements documents, but the development manager has not yet signed off on the requirements because she has raised some minor questions recently that are related to the clarification of requirements. The questions/issues are still open. The project manager had a discussion with the development manager when the requirements analysis had finished, and they agreed that estimates of the development team would be ready in one to two weeks. This did not happen. In the meantime, QA has already provided their estimates and they are asking about the timelines when they should be ready with the resources as well as the test plan, test case, and test data for the testing to begin. The PM has no idea about the end date for the development and unit testing. Customers and business users are also putting pressure on the PM to provide definitive dates along with expected time and cost to complete the project.

At the end of the third week, the PM schedules a meeting with the development lead and the development manager to discuss the estimates because the development manager had asked to provide an extra week at the end of the second week after requirements finished. In the meeting, the PM finds out that the development manager is not fully prepared with the effort estimates. She presents the effort estimates but does not sound very confident; she says her team has reviewed the requirements and has understood but she herself wants to review everything very thoroughly before committing anything. Apart from that, she does not provide any timelines to the PM with respect to the completion of design or for the start and finish of development tasks. When asked the reason for not providing these timelines, she says she cannot provide them until all the open questions of the requirements are answered properly. She is apprehensive because, in the past, the moment she revealed the dates, people considered that as concrete and the expectations were set accordingly. The PM assures her that he will set the expectation about the dates to customers and other stakeholders accordingly, but he needs to understand some tentative timelines so that he can make critical decisions, including resource planning. Additionally, he also states that she can assume that open items will be closed by the following week and she should provide the timelines based on that assumption. But she does not agree to that. The PM becomes very frustrated and starts arguing that the project does not work this way. He argues that he has to know the estimates about cost and schedule at different stages of the project, whether or not they are final; the degree of confidence on the estimate may be low during initial stages. The development manager says she will not work that way. The meeting does not go very well, but they do agree to meet again soon; however, the development manager does not provide any expected time when they can meet.

Issues to Examine: Analyze the situation and prepare a list of issues with regard to the process of communication that you think might be the cause of this dispute. If you were the arbitrator in that meeting, what would have been your advice to each party? If you were the PM, what would have been your next steps after such a meeting?

31. **Where Is the Boundary?:** A product development project is being executed in two phases. Currently, phase 1 is finished and phase 2 has just started. The project organization is almost the same as that in phase 1, except for the lead project manager. You have joined the organization recently to replace the lead project manager. After a couple of weeks, you observe that the project team is working on issues reported on the product developed a long time back in phase 1. As per the organization's process, any defect reported for the product after one month of its release will be fixed by the operation team, not the project team. In this case, users reported the defects to the project team instead of the operations team. The project team is being nice to the business users so they are fixing the defects. Until now, your previous project manager was logging the issues in the project issue list and was tracking them on a weekly basis. Phase 2 is not sufficiently budgeted because phase 1 overspent and those valuable dollars were deducted from the phase 2 budget.

Issues to Examine: List reasons behind the cause of problems described above. How should you proceed to put a check on overspending? What should you do to ensure that the project team focuses on the project work and the non-project operations/maintenance work gets diverted to the proper organization where it can be handled in the best possible way?

32. **Conflict Within the Team:** Two very critical resources on your project do not get along very well. Their work requires interaction between them. Because their fighting comes into the open whenever they interact, it has become very difficult to make progress. It is creating a nuisance in the

project. They are very skilled resources and cannot be easily replaced. In general, both resources get along well with other team members. Neither of them reports directly to you; each reports to a different functional manager. **Issues to Examine:** How would you tackle this situation in the short term and in the long term? Which communication tool/media should you use, and which communication tool/media should you definitely avoid?

33. **Everchanging Schedule:** You are the PM of a software development project. The implementation date of the project has shifted at least three times in the past, and for different reasons each time. Business users are very frustrated and this has been escalated to top management. They have lost faith, so the last time they asked you to provide a date after considering all the risks and issues and after taking into account the different factors affecting the project. You met with the team members and after much deliberation and due diligence, you presented a new date to the users and stakeholders. You also mentioned the assumptions, risks, as well as risk response plans. The project is in the user acceptance testing (UAT) stage with five major open defects. Everything went well and the UAT finished before the new proposed time. The team prepared for the production implementation. However, the day before implementation, the technical lead notifies you that a software client is not present in the production environment, so one of the components will not work. It takes about one to two weeks to get the client loaded once the request is raised. This will delay the production implementation and the date will be missed again.

    Issues to Examine: How would you prepare the response for the stakeholders? Would you consult your boss and other concerned executives in your organization for preparing and blessing the response? How would you break the news and who should you blame for missing this deadline?

34. **Whiny Customer:** One of the subject matter experts (SMEs) often complains that SME time is not being utilized properly on this project. There are three technicians and analysts on the project who often need to interact with the SME for questions and clarifications. You, as the PM, also have a standing meeting with the SME, technicians, and the analysts together, where you discuss various open items and issues on a weekly basis. Technicians and analysts have separate meetings with the SMEs throughout the week as and when they require. The SME suggests that there should be just one or two meetings throughout the week, as too many meetings are overkill for her and leave no time for her other commitments. At the same time, the analysts complain that the SME does not respond to their emails on time and the response is often not clear enough so they need to meet frequently. The meeting has to happen immediately; otherwise, there will be delays. The SME also complains that the analysts are not experienced and skilled enough to understand the subject matter easily. They need direction and guidance and so she wants you to be present at all meetings that happen between the analysts

and the SME. You do not have enough time to attend all these meetings. The SME has escalated this issue to senior management.

Issues to Examine: How would you resolve this conflict? Analyze the symptoms of the problem, get to the root cause of the issue, and suggest steps that the PM should take to set a protocol to resolve the above-mentioned conflicts.

35. **Fussy Stakeholder:** Consider that the above-mentioned SME is quite finicky. She is very hard to please, and she reports issues with everything and often escalates matters, which the project team finds unhealthy. On occasion, she has even passed the buck after failures. She has a wealth of knowledge on specialized matters, so you cannot do away with her service. But the team members find it extremely difficult to work with her. She has a very good rapport with senior management because of her subject matter expertise, vast knowledge, and hard work. This makes the situation even trickier.

Issues to Examine: How should you sort out this issue so that team members work in a fearless and healthy environment? You also must be very careful not to lose the valuable expertise of the SME.

36. **Disgruntled Employee:** One fine morning you find out that the lead engineer of the project is very upset, the reason being that he received an average rating in the annual employee appraisal, the result of which was declared just this morning. He is skillful, understands his job well, is knowledgeable, is hard working, and is a key resource on the project. He appears to be upset with his functional manager and looks demotivated. He was supposed to take care of some critical tasks first thing this morning, has not done this yet, and has informed you that he is leaving for the day. You have suggested that he talk to his reporting manager about the appraisal ratings and find out why he got the rating that he did and what he (the engineer) can do to improve the rating next time. The engineer replies that the same thing also happened in his previous appraisal. He had talked to his manager, but did not get a satisfactory answer to his questions, so he does not want to talk to him any more on this subject. Your project is at a very critical stage where any lapse from the lead engineer will adversely impact the project.

Issues to Examine: How should you handle this situation from a communication management and human resource management perspective? You have to ensure that the employees working on your project are highly motivated, there is a healthy working environment in the project, and the project work is not impacted by human resource management issues. List the steps you should take as the PM.

37. **Ways to Make Yourself Heard:** You are managing a very challenging project. Major challenges on the project include (1) unrealistic timelines set by the customer and accepted by senior management; (2) inexperienced team members; and (3) external dependencies. You created the project management plan and also identified ways to overcome these challenges. As part of the risk and issue management exercise, you identified major risks that might impede your abilities to overcome the challenges. You need a lot of senior management support for the execution of the risk response plans. The risk register was updated and communicated to the stakeholders, including senior management of

the organization. You did not hear from anyone for three days, so you informed them through email, communicating the major issues and what you are expecting from senior management. You stated the impact, ways to resolve the issues, by what date the action should be taken, etc. Apparently, nobody responded to your email. You mentioned these risks and issues in your weekly project status report, but somehow you get the feeling that they are falling on deaf ears.

Issues to Examine: What should you do next from a communication management perspective? What could have been done differently to achieve a better result?

38. **Communication Breakdown:** You are the PM of a software development project. The project has a matrix organization where nobody reports directly to you. All the human resources report to their respective functional managers belonging to different departments and you report to the PMO. There are two QA resources working on the project. One finished his test script two weeks ago and the second person is supposed to finish it by today. When you inquire as to the status today after a gap of about a week, the second QA resource says that he is allocated to another project for a week. So, there is no progress since last week. You are surprised as well as upset by this.

Issues to Examine: What should you do next? Should the matter be escalated? If yes, then how? Should you complain about the QA resource to his manager, or should you complain about the QA manager himself? Where does the issue lie? Why is there a breakdown in communication?

39. **Organization's Politics:** You are managing a decommissioning project. This is a different kind of experience for you. You prepared a plan for ramping down the resources over time, and you are revisiting that ramp-down plan every two weeks based on the remaining work, changes in the project variables, and changes to the assumptions. Rightfully, the organization is moving out vital and experienced resources from this project and engaging them on other strategic projects. You still have a lot of work left in the project, but one of your challenges is retaining good resources and acquiring good resources on time. Good resources are being replaced by not-so-skilled ones because the organization wants to focus on other strategic projects that will bear revenue for the organization in the future. Suddenly you receive notification about three critical defects in one of the products the organization had supplied to the customer. The customer also warns that if the defects in the product are not fixed in one month, they will take the matter to court. Failing to oblige the customer, your organization may have to pay a hefty fine. The fix requires a dedicated resource for three weeks. To address the issue, you write a change control to secure extra budget and resources on an immediate basis. The change control is submitted to the project steering committee; every member of the committee approves it immediately—except for one member who represents the organization that owns the required resources. After working in the organization for a long time, you understand the politics of the organization and you are not at all surprised by the response (or lack thereof) of that person. After waiting for three days for the response, you reach out to that approver, who, in turn, responds by saying that she does not have the authority to get additional

resources for this work and asks you to utilize your existing resources to get the work done. The project is executing only the critical work required to meet the contractual agreements and is already short of sufficient numbers and quality of resources to meet these minimum needs.

Issues to Examine: This is a tricky situation. Should you sit back and do nothing because you have raised this issue through various communication channels (emails to all concerned, change control, updated issue list, and status report)? Should you hold a meeting of the steering committee to discuss this issue by making everyone clearly aware of the impact? Discussing the matter by bringing everyone to the same table might spur constructive dialogue. Or, should you reach out to the head of the department that owns the resource group to explain your situation and to request the resource? The environment is very political and there is always a tussle between the business group and the functional departments. You should handle the situation in such a way that it does not harm your reputation and at the same time ensures that the organization takes an informed decision on the issue. You should not end up in the bad books of any one of the senior executives. You may be passionate about the project, but you cannot afford to be vitriolic for getting the points across. Remember: The PM is not always successful by getting the work done "by hook or by crook." List the communication tools you would use to handle this situation in the most appropriate manner.

40. **Why So Many Reports?:** You spend more than an hour every week diligently preparing the weekly project status report and distributing it to all project stakeholders. You have not received a single feedback or question from anyone in the past two months—which seems bizarre to you. Some executives ask you from time to time to provide them with reports in different formats. The executives get a copy of the weekly project status report, and had they gone through the report, they would not have asked for another report. You are very nice to the stakeholders, particularly those at the executive level, so you generate reports as per their demands.

Issues to Examine: What might be the reasons behind people not reading your weekly status report? What should be done to reduce the demand of ad-hoc reports so that the PM will not have to rework the same information to produce multiple reports for different people on different occasions?

41. **Estimates Are Not Appropriate:** Work estimation is a very tricky job that requires lots of input and considerations. Most people generally do not understand the concept of the timing when estimations need to be done, the degree of variation that should be expected, and how the variations need to be interpreted and handled. Your new organization has a very poor estimation process and people have only a vague understanding of project estimation. You as an expert project manager understand that work estimation is done by considering past experiences of the similar work, expert advice, current resource skill level for a similar task, elements of risk involved in the current project related to the particular work, etc. You are the PM for a software development project. The OOM estimate (E1) is available for the project at the beginning. Once the requirements document is complete, you ask the technical lead to provide you with an estimate of the development work. The estimate provided by the technical

lead appears very low. So, you ask her the method used by the lead in coming up with the estimates. You also ask her to list the assumptions she considered while preparing the estimate. You want to validate the assumptions now and at subsequent stages in the project. Assumptions should always be mentioned with all the estimates and plans. The technical lead explains to you that she used the Simple-Medium-Complex (SMC) model for the work estimation and has presented you with the figure that she obtained from the estimation tool.

Issues to Examine: The estimation tool referred to by the technical lead is the enterprisewide standard used in every project of the organization. So, should you readily accept the output of the tool? Should the tool be driving the people, or should people be driving the tool? The technical lead is more technically qualified than you and knows her job better than you do, so should you be questioning the estimation of the development work done by an expert?

42. **Again Politics?:** Schedule and cost are the two prominent causes of contention in any project. The IT project that you manage is currently in the development phase. You have collected the cost and time estimates from the development team after the design phase finished. The estimates are way below the expectations of the business unit owning this project. That is, the cost estimate is very high, and the schedule is longer than anticipated in the beginning. After receiving the estimate, you negotiate with the development manager to get the best resources engaged on the project to improve cost and timelines. However, the revised estimate is also very far from the expectation of the business group. You are planning to have a meeting with the development unit head, development manager, and the business leads so that everyone has an opportunity to discuss the reason(s) behind the high estimates and ways to optimize those estimates. Business leads fear that the development team is not giving proper attention to this project and is not engaging its best resources on this project. Even before you could bring everyone to the table, the business head calls the development head and complains about the high estimates and requests to use the best resources on the project. The development head thinks that the project manager (you) is passing all the little internal information to the business group, so he is not very happy with you. The environment is very political.

Issues to Examine: You should not jeopardize your relationships with any group; neither should you fall prey to the organization's politics. You understand that in order to manage the project well, you need full support from every unit. Understanding the organization's politics is critical to the success of a PM. Good communication is the key to good interpersonal relationships and to get the work done in a harmonious environment. Communication skills are also vital for negotiations. Analyze the above situation and suggest what should have been done differently by the PM to avoid the situation? Could this situation have been avoided? How should the situation be tackled to restore a good relationship with the development head and to ensure that the project is not adversely impacted because of the conflict and friction.

43. Crisis: The WBS (work breakdown structure) is a vital tool for planning, estimation, and communication. Unless you understand all the constituent activities of the work, it is difficult to provide an estimate with a high degree of confidence. The WBS from a previous project is being used in your current project. It has been reviewed, for suitability for the current project, by all the subject matter experts assigned to the project and everyone has blessed it—with some modifications. Effort and schedule estimation was done as per the detailed WBS and the deployment date was communicated to the client accordingly. The customer, in turn, promised the launch of the product accordingly in the marketplace. This is a six-month project. Everything goes very well until quality testing starts in the fifth month. A major defect is discovered in the testing. Upon thorough investigation, it is established that the WBS is missing a major activity. Fixing the defect by performing the new activity will push the date out by one month. This will have a huge impact on your customer's reputation in the marketplace. Some of the stakeholders in your organization begin to panic after hearing this news.

Issues to Examine: What should be your immediate priority in light of this situation? How should you plan communication with the customer? Who should break the news, and how should it be communicated? Remember: everything depends on the way the fact is communicated.

Index

A

Acceptance criteria, 135
Action item log, 138, 139f, 140–142
Agenda, meeting, 66, 69–70, 71, 159

B

Bar charts, 95
Budgeting
    cost management plan, 31
    order of magnitude, 38, 73, 163

C

Cause and effect diagram, 102–103
Change management plan, 38–39
Change request document, 60–62, 163
Charts. *See specific chart types*
Closure report, project, 72–74
Column charts, 95–96
Communication management plan
    communication matrix (*see*
        Communication matrix)
    consistency issues, 167
    elements of, 36
    overview, 35–36
    project manager's role, 36–37
Communication matrix, 36, 124, 125f
Communications, 164–165
    breakdowns in, 2, 164, 169–170, 175
    consistency, 167
    defining, 3
    importance, 1–2
    negotiation, 164–165
    nonverbal, 6
    project environment, in (*see* Project
        communications)
    verbal, 6
    written, 6
Competition
    global, 44
    quality, importance of, 44–45
Configuration management (CM) plan
    audit, 54–55
    elements of, 53
    overview, 52–53
    process flow, 54
    scope, 52–53
Control chart
    attribute data, 106, 107
    common causes, 105–106
    lower control limit, 106
    out-of-control indicators, interpreting,
        108–109
    overview, 104–105
    procedure for use, 107–108
    special causes, 106
    stable process overview, 105
    upper control limit, 106
    usage, 105
    variable data, 106, 107
Cost management plan
    cost budgeting, 31
    cost control, 32
    cost estimation, 30–31
    cost reporting, 32
    cost trackers, 33f
    Earned Value Technique (*see* Earned
        Value Technique (EVT))
Crosby, Philip, 43

D

Dashboard, project, 142–144
Decision tree diagram, 113–116
Defect management plan

costs of defects, 42
defect life cycle, 41
defect prevention, 42–43
overview, 39, 41
tools for, 41–42
Drucker, Peter, 2, 43

E

Earned Value Technique (EVT), 32, 34
Einstein, Albert, 158
Emails
attachments, 81–82
communication channel, as, 80–81
do's of communication, 79–80
don'ts of communication, 77–78
ease of reading, 76
follow-ups, use for, 80
general etiquette, 76–77
importance to business, 11–12
sample messages, 78
Environmental management plan (EMP),
59–60

F

Flowcharts, 91–93

G

Gantt charts
customization, 86
example, 88*f*, 89*f*, 90*f*
information in, 87
organization of, 86–87
popularity, 86
schedules, for, 29–30, 86–87

H

Histograms
resource type, 96–97, 98*f*
usage, 95
Human resources (HR) management plan,
34–35, 174

I

ISO 9000, 43
Issue log, 138, 139*f*, 140–142

J

Joseph, Juran, 43

K

Kickoff meeting agenda, project, 19–21, 165
Knowledge areas, project management, 9
Knowledge management (KM) plan, 55–57,
162

L

Lessons learned document, 74–76
Line chart, 98–99

M

Milestone report, 65–66, 67–68*f*
Minutes, meeting, 66, 70–72
MS PowerPoint, 82–84
MS Project, 27, 28

O

Organization breakdown structure (OBS),
119–120
Organization chart, 109–111

P

Pareto chart, 100–102
Peter, Tom, 2
Pie chart, 103–104
Pivot chart, 156*f*
Pivot table, 144, 146, 147*f*, 148–149*f*, 150–152*f*,
153–155*f*
PowerPoint, MS, 82–84
Process defect matrix, 137*f*
Process groups, project management
closing, 8–9
executing, 8
initiation, 8
monitoring and control, 8–9
planning, 8
Procurement management plan, 50–52
Project charter, 11
authorization of project, 14–15
defining, 12
fluid (*versus* static), 14
information in, 12–14
project scope document, 12

Project communications. *See also*
Communications
barriers to, 5
channel, 4
decoding, 5
encoding, 5
execution, 6
filtering, 5
formal, 4
importance, 2
informal, 4
interpersonal, 3–4
links within, 5–6
management plan (*see* Communication
management plan)
message, 4
noise, 5
planning, 6
problem prevention, 7–8
public/community, with, 4
receiver, 4
relationship building, 6–7
sender, 4
text-based tools, 11–12
unnecessary, 37
Project dashboard, 142–144, 145*f*
Project initiation document (PID), 11, 160
elements of, 17–18
overview, 17
purpose of, 18–19
Project kickoff meeting agenda, 19–21, 165
Project management plan, 11
defining, 21–22
integrated project plan, 22
overview, 21
progressive elaboration, 24
project strategies as part of, 22–23
rolling wave planning, 24
Project management, defining, 157–158
Project team roster, 124, 126, 127*f*

Q

Quality assurance, 24
measurements, 44
Quality control, 44
Quality management plan
delegation of management portion, 24
lack of, consequences of, 45–46
overview, 43
perspectives on, 43
Quality matrix, 45, 135–138

R

Resource histogram, 96–97, 98*f*
Responsibility assignment matrix (RAM),
119–122
Risk management plan
complexity of, 129
defining risk, 46
elements of, 47–48
importance of, 46–47
opportunity, strategies for, 49, 50
overview, 46
risk probability-impact matrix (*see* Risk
probability-impact matrix)
risk register (*see* Risk register)
risk *versus* issue, 138, 141–42
threat, strategies for, 48–49, 50
Risk probability-impact matrix, 126, 128–129
Risk register, 174–175
communication tool, 129–130
creation, timing of, 130
low *versus* high score risks, 130, 132
overview, 129
requirements traceability matrix, 132,
133*f*, 134–135
sample, 131*f*
Role and responsibility matrix, 122–124
Rolling wave planning, 24
Run chart, 98–99
Run-sequence plot, 98–99

S

S curves, 93–95
Sarbanes-Oxley checkpoints, 164
Scenarios for test-based tools
agendas for better meetings, 159
baseline and variation tolerance, 163
best option of charts, etc., 167
boundaries and phases, 172
change requests, 163
communication breakdowns, 164, 175
communication consistency, 167
confusion, clarifying, 168
creative hat, need for, 161–162
crisis, 178
difficult customers, 173–174
disputes, 170–172
follow-up issues, 163
gaps in responsibility assignments, 169
human resources issues, 174

information overdose *versus* information
    scarcity, 162
knowledge management, 162
leak prevention, 169
list preparation, 169
negotiation, 164–165
one-on-one with senior executives, 170
organization politics, 175–176, 177–178
panic scenario, 170
poorly defined scope, 161
problem-solving tool, 166–167
progress reports, 160
project planning, 160–161
recalcitrant customers, 160
reports, 169–170, 176
responsibilities, 168–169, 169
risk, 174–175
scheduling changes, 173
senior management issues, 165
skillsets, 169
smart communications, 164–165
team conflicts, 172–173
termination, early, 160
triple constraint, 161
unknown/unplanned event, 159
work breakdown structure (WBS), 178
work estimation, 176–177
Schedule management plan
changes, managing, 173
elements of, 26–27
Gantt charts (*see* Gantt charts)
interconnectedness of elements of, 28–29
milestone dates, 27
overview, 26
reporting tools, 117–118
tasks, 28–29
templates, 27
timelines, 27–28
Scope management plan
alternative identification, 26
analysis tools, 26
configuration management system, 26
defining, 24–25

elements of, 25
forms, 25
guidelines, 25
product analysis, 25
standards, 26
templates, 25
Six Sigma
quality, definition of, 43
Statement of Work (SOW), 11
contents, 15–16
defining, 15
length of, 16
planning for, 16–17
project charter, as part of, 12
purpose of, 18–19
usage as communication tool, 17
Status report, project
application areas, 63–64
elements of, 62–63
importance, 62
overview, 62
tips for creating, 64–65

T

Total Quality Management (TQM), 136
Transition plan, 57–58

V

Visual aids, 82. *See also* MS PowerPoint
charts (*see specific chart types*)
diagrams (*see specific diagram types*)
Visual Source Safe, 26

W

Work breakdown structure (WBS), 111–112,
    178
responsibility assignment matrix,
    relationship between, 119–120
Work estimation, 176–177

Milton Keynes UK
Ingram Content Group UK Ltd.
UKHW040057071024
449327UK00019B/611

9 780367 384326